GARLAND STUDIES IN

ENTREPRENEURSHIP

edited by

STUART BRUCHEY
UNIVERSITY OF MAINE

A GARLAND SERIES

INNOVATION AND GROWTH IN AN AFRICAN AMERICAN OWNED BUSINESS

GWENDOLYN POWELL TODD

GARLAND PUBLISHING, Inc.
New York & London / 1996

Library of Congress Cataloging-in-Publication Data

Todd, Gwendolyn Powell, 1947–
    Innovation and growth in an African American owned
business / Gwendolyn Powell Todd.
        p.   cm. — (Garland studies in entrepreneurship)
    Includes bibliographical references and index.
    ISBN 0-8153-2598-3 (alk. paper)
    1. Don Todd Associates. 2. Afro-American business
enterprises—Management. 3. Small business—United States—
Management. 4. Entrepreneurship—United States.   I. Title.
II. Series.
HD62.7.T63 1996
658'.0089'96073—dc2   96-41528

Printed on acid-free, 250-year-life paper
Manufactured in the United States of America

For Donald J. Todd, P.E.,

and the DTA staff

Table of Contents

List of Illustrations

PREFACE

As an African American doctoral student in organization and leadership, I searched for the presentation of African American firms in the study of organizations, management, leadership, and strategic planning. I looked for African American firms in textbooks and case study materials. I found none. I polled seven of my colleagues who possessed advanced business or organizational degrees from some of the most prestigious universities in this country, and found that none had studied a black-owned firm. The singular exception was a presentation by entrepreneur Donald J. Todd in the management class taught by Dr. Allen Calvin at the University of San Francisco (USF).

Paradoxically, the literature is inundated with research demonstrating the need for positive role models who illustrate behavior patterns that others can imitate. Role models are particularly important as they demonstrate those areas where "like" people can succeed. It follows then, that if African Americans do not *see* black entrepreneurs, they are less likely to imitate entrepreneurial behavior. Role modeling is critical if African Americans are to successfully start and maintain businesses. The paucity of literature regarding black entrepreneurship fueled my desire to study the topic, and the suggestion of Dr. Anita DeFrantz, a professor at USF, that I focus on that which I experienced daily—my work with an African American entrepreneurship—solidified that desire. Several areas of possible research surfaced.

I have worked in businesses owned by African Americans, and by others under European American proprietorship. I sensed a difference in the challenges I faced as an administrator in these businesses. Discussions with black colleagues confirmed my perceptions. The question arose: Were these challenges real, or falsely perceived? There were no studies available addressing specific challenges of black-owned businesses, or successful solutions to problems unique to black businesses.

The absence of blacks in the literature puzzled me and raised additional questions: Does this absence imply that other ethnic groups, including European Americans, cannot learn from the management strategies of black entrepreneurs? Are there not some principles executed well by African Americans that are generalizable to all businesses?

The lack of answers to these, and other questions, served as the impetus for my study of an African American-owned firm, Don Todd Associates (DTA). I chose not to study the black entrepreneur, but rather to carefully study the founding and development of the organization and management style; and to discover which management principles and strategies were used by this black entrepreneur to create a successful business.

While some encouraged me to compare an African American-owned firm with that of another ethnic group, my advisor, Dr. Robert Lamp, and I felt that African Americans need in-depth studies of our positive behaviors and successes. My desire was to present a complete set of data on one African American firm that could later be compared with studies of other firms, regardless of ethnicity. Comparing the results of two ethnic groups would have diluted the focus of the study.

A secondary emphasis evolved as it became clear that DTA has developed and maintained a multi-ethnic staff. This diversity has been present for years, and since diversity is such an important issue in the business arena, it deserved further exploration. While many large organizations are still trying to achieve diversity, and those few who have some degree of diversity struggle to manage it, how did DTA, a mid-size, African American-owned firm, achieve such a high level of diversity? Others are attempting to achieve an organizational culture that DTA has maintained for over 17 years. Other intriguing questions were: How did the members of these ethnic groups feel about the multi-ethnicity of the firm? Did the multi-ethnicity of the firm affect the success or failure of the firm?

How a black firm has sustained itself through 17 years of challenges and has managed to accomplish such a culture is a story worth telling. My hope is that African Americans of all ages and stages will read this study and be inspired and challenged to develop business, or to solidify existing ones. I also hope that other ethnic groups will find solutions to issues they have been pondering . . . that they will find solutions from an African American-owned firm.

Gwendolyn Powell Todd
San Francisco
May 1996

ACKNOWLEDGMENTS

It is with sincere appreciation that I thank all the people who have helped me reach this goal. I received many prayers and strong encouragement. My committee, Drs. Lamp, Calvin, and DeFrantz provided excellent direction.

Many thanks go to the DTA employees. Without their cooperation, support, and enthusiasm, this research could not have been completed.

I am indebted to the friends and family members who prayed for me and supported me in many different ways. It is not possible to acknowledge each of them, but I am deeply grateful to Kathleen Thurman and Joy Acevedo, who have been invaluable supporters. I especially thank my parents, Lee and Gentle Powell, who were my first role models and taught me to constantly excel. They remain an inspiration to me and an unending source of guidance.

Completing the study and this book would not have been possible without the support of my loving husband, Don. He supported me by giving me the freedom to study, listening to all my "stories," and encouraging me when things became difficult. As my business and spiritual partner, Don helped to maintain balance in our lives.

Last, but never least, I thank God for His many blessings.

> Trust in the Lord with all thine heart; and lean not to thine own understanding.
>
> In all thy ways acknowledge Him, and He shall direct thy paths.
>
> Proverbs 3:5-6
> KJV

Innovation and Growth in an African American Owned Business

I

Don Todd Associates, Inc.: Challenges to the Business

WHY STUDY DTA?

Don Todd Associates, Inc. (DTA), an African American-owned construction management firm, was founded in 1977 by Donald J. Todd. The firm has 120 employees and three offices: New York City; Cherry Hill, New Jersey; and corporate headquarters in San Francisco. DTA ranks #58 in the top one hundred Construction Management (CM) firms (gross sales),[1] has a multi-ethnic staff, and has maintained profitability during the national economic recession.

DTA faces many challenges. The firm's primary sources of work are public works and infrastructure projects. As such, DTA faces increasingly shrinking markets. Federal government funding for these projects is in a state of decline. *Engineering News Record* (ENR) reports that "Already pinched, construction and environmental programs will continue to be pressed by the new deficit reduction law, which basically freezes domestic programs from 1995–1998."[2] ENR also reports that California construction awards increased by only 1 percent from 1992–1993.[3]

DTA encounters the additional challenge of having lost its disadvantaged minority business status by exceeding the gross revenue limit for affirmative action programs. This is problematic in that many agencies and larger firms view minorities as being disadvantaged and only wish to utilize minority firms if those firms fulfill affirmative action goals.

Other obstacles include increased competition from new businesses formed by individuals laid off from larger companies; the expansion into CM of small firms that have traditionally provided other architectural or engineering services; competition with large CM firms for smaller projects; the move of multi-national firms to metropolitan areas; and the migration of businesses and related construction work from the San Francisco Bay area. Clients are requiring more attention and communication, faster response, a smaller scope of work, and lower fees. ENR states, "Design fees have been flat since 1985 and declining since 1991."[4] As a result, DTA experienced a profit decline during the years 1990–1993.[5] Finally, DTA's President and Founder, Donald J. Todd, P.E., is planning to retire in five years and succession planning is required.

Is DTA equipped to deal with the organizational, financial and management issues necessary to plan a successful future? Due to the paucity of research on African American businesses and CM firms, DTA must look within to meet these external and internal challenges.

The purpose of this research was to conduct an in-depth case study of Don Todd Associates. The analysis would determine if DTA is equipped with the organizational, financial, and management information necessary to plan a successful future. An additional purpose was to expand the body of knowledge regarding African American entrepreneurial organizations.

BACKGROUND AND NEED FOR THE STUDY

Businesses are the core of the economy, and consequently it is important that businesses of all types continue to flourish. It has been difficult for businesses to grow and prosper during the recent economic recession. Most businesses in the construction industry have been struggling to avoid demise. In California, the construction market declined 45 percent from 1989–1993.[6] This decline in available design and construction projects led many firms in the industry to reduce their staffs by 25 to 75 percent and to reduce principal salaries by as much as 50 percent.[7] Turner Construction is a multi-national firm, ranked 15th among ENR's Top 400 U.S. contractors in 1993, and the nation's second-largest building contractor. A loss of $6.2 million in 1993 prompted them to "right size," by merging smaller offices into larger regional ones and reducing staff by 125 to 150 people.[8]

The intensity of the struggle increases significantly for the African American-owned business. In addition to the usual problems associated with market decline, African American-owned firms encounter inequitable business practices and management and leadership difficulties leading to demise. One discriminatory practice is the difficulty African American-owned firms have accessing capital. Even an established business may need to increase capital in order to support the organization during a time when creditors are slow paying or when costs are legitimately increasing. African American entrepreneurs often find that financial institutions do not support the expansion of their credit lines. Closing the door to capital access has been one of the real problems for black businesses.[9]

Black-owned businesses find more success in cities with black mayors.[10] New York City is an example. Mayor David Dinkins allowed city procurement staff to develop a practice of awarding contracts to minority and women-owned businesses if their bids were within 10 percent of the lowest offer. Under this program, established in August of 1992, minority and women-owned businesses doubled their share of city contracts. Less than one month after Rudolph Giuliani succeeded Mayor Dinkins, Mayor Giuliani eliminated the nation's largest city's minority contracting program.[11]

> The decision to cancel the controversial bid preference program proves how fragile many local minority contracting programs are. Since the Supreme Court's Croson decision in 1989 requiring municipalities to prove evidence of past discrimination, local and state set-aside programs have come under close scrutiny.[12]

Other forms of affirmative action also create problems for growing entrepreneurial enterprises. As minority firms grow and revenues surpass affirmative action goals, they must compete with large, long established firms with an excess of capital, resources and experience. This becomes an impossible task for some minority firms.

Succession planning should be a part of the strategic planning for any entrepreneurial firm. However, African American firms are often so busy trying to maintain profitability that there is little time for succession planning. This was the case for the principals of the black-owned securities firm of Daniels and Bell.[13] When Trevor Bell unexpectedly died of a heart attack in 1988, the $15 million company was placed in the hands of his son, Darryl Bell, who was unfamiliar with the business. The courts have since required Daniels and Bell to terminate or dispose of itself in order to pay its outstanding debts. Similarly, when one of the most successful African American entrepreneurs of our time, Reginald Lewis, died of brain cancer there was no clear succession plan. Shortly before Lewis died he appointed his half brother, Jean Fugett, Jr., to lead the company. The company struggled, Fugett resigned, and Loida Lewis, widow of Reginald Lewis, assumed the company's leadership.[14]

Clearly, these are all issues that DTA is currently facing. In order to avoid the fate of the companies mentioned here, an analysis of the firm was needed. In addition, if the firm has faced some of these or other problems and successfully met the challenges, knowledge of this process would be helpful for other firms. Dr. Dennis Kimbro indicated that, although there are approximately 442,000 African American firms in America, he knew of only one or two case studies.[15] Many African Americans complete MBA and other business programs never having studied a minority business. This lack of representation in the literature presents a poor picture of what African Americans can become.[16] Clearly, the paucity of literature available on African American firms needs to be rectified in order that future and current African American entrepreneurs have appropriate models to study.

CONCEPTUAL FRAMEWORK FOR THE STUDY

As an African American-owned firm, Don Todd Associates, Inc. (DTA) is facing several internal and external threats. A review of the organizational literature revealed three appropriate approaches to the examination of an organization. The dynamic organizational model was chosen for use in this study.

The first model is cross sectional and analyzes an organization at a given point in time.[17] This model would require the researcher to examine DTA at its current level of functioning only. The cross sectional model would not allow DTA to study and take advantage of its successful history, nor provide the organization with enough information to make major decisions.

The second model provides a longitudinal study that reviews the organization's maturational process. Cameron and Quinn integrate nine such life cycle models into one model.[18] They indicate four major stages of an organization: the entrepreneurial stage, collectivity stage, formalization and control stage, and elaboration of structure stage. While this model would give the organization more information than the cross sectional model, it does not allow organizations to be flexible and make adjustments over time. Also, organizations may not fall within these distinct phases. It also would not account for the decision making process of the organization.

The third model is the dynamic organizational model, which indicates that organizations are constantly changing. Tichy's Technical, Political and Cultural (TPC) framework states that organizational change and growth can best be described by observing how an organization responds to uncertainties with regard to internal and external environmental threats, opportunities, organization size, or technological trends.[19] He maintains that these threats cause problems in the organizational system by affecting one of three subsystems: technical; political; or cultural. Since DTA is currently experiencing major internal and external environmental threats, it is most appropriate to utilize this model to examine the organization.

The technical subsystem consists of the social, financial, and technical resources. Problems with production uncertainties must be resolved if the organization is to adjust and survive. Problems are solved by goal setting, strategy formulation, organizational design, and the design of management systems.

The political subsystem is concerned with allocation of power and resources. In this subsystem it is decided who determines how to use resources and how issues will be resolved. The uses of the organization and recipient(s) of the rewards are also determined.

Finally, the cultural subsystem determines what values are held by what people. Beliefs, values, objectives, and interpretations hold organizations together. If there are divergent beliefs, problems will arise which must be resolved if the organization is to survive.

To determine if there are problems in the technical, cultural or political subsystems of an organization, an examination of eight organizational dimensions must take place. These "management tools" are:

1. Input
    - History of the organization—critical events, identifiable phases of development, service mix history of the organization.
    - Environment of the organization—With whom or what is the organization interdependent upon for goods, services, information and influence? How fluid and predictable is environmental change?
    - Organizational resources—What capital does the organization control? What is the state of the technical capability? What are the "people resources"?

2. Mission/Strategy/Objectives
    - Mission—What is the formal mission, and how is it formulated? How do the members describe it?
    - Strategy—Is there a formal strategy, and how was it determined? How do the members perceive it?
    - What are the goals of the organization as perceived by key staff and members?

3. Tasks
    - What are the basic tasks; who performs them; how are they interrelated; what is their nature and the expertise required?

4. Prescribed Organization Analysis
    - Differentiation—How is the organization differentiated vertically, horizontally, and spatially? What is the distribution of budgets, personnel, and tasks? What are the characteristics of individual units?
    - Integration—What is the overall configuration of the organization?

5. People Analysis
    - Demographic characteristics of the staff—ethnicity, educational level, professional certifications and personal characteristics of the staff.

- Managerial styles of key staff—How participative and flexible is management? What is the level of mutual respect, support and trust between management and staff?
- Motivational forces driving staff—What are the values of the staff and how does that match what they get? How do staff perceive their own ability to control their effectiveness?

6. Organizational Processes Analysis
   - Communication style—How open is communication? How effective is the communication at various levels?
   - Decision making style—What is the basic mode of decision making in the organization? Are there different modes of decision making for different issues?

7. Emergent Organization Analysis
   - What is the overall informal organization? Who shares information with whom and who influences whom regarding what issues?
   - Which coalitions are formed? Are there recognizable groups of people who cooperate in order to exert influence? If so, around what issues?
   - What cliques exist? Are there durable clusters of friends within the organization?

8. Output Analysis
   - Degree of goal optimization—To what degree are resources being applied toward the attainment of goals? Is there a clear relationship between the amount of resources spent on the various goals and the importance of the goal? Are goals adjusted with environmental changes? Are goals achieved?
   - Behavioral impacts of the organization—How satisfied are members with their work, each other, their careers?

The interaction of these eight dimensions function in an open systems model as seen in figure 1.

Figure 1: Open Systems Model

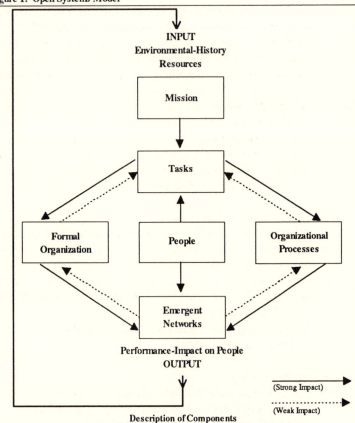

Description of Components

Mission/Strategy: This includes the ogranization's reason for being, its basic approach to carrying out its mission, its strategy, and its criteria for effectiveness.

Tasks: This refers to the technology by which the organization's work is accomplished.

People: This includes the characteristics of the members of the organization including background, motivational patterns, managerial style.

Formal Organization: This refers to the explicitly designed social structure of the organization. It includes the organization of subunits, communication and authority networks, as well as structural mechanisms for integrating the organization

Organization Process: These are the mechanisms (communication, decision making, conflict management, control, and reward) which enable the formal organization to carry out the dynamics of work.

Emergent Networks: These are the structures and processes which, although not planned or formally prescribed, inevitably emerge in the organization.

(Source: Tichy, 1983, p.96. Managing Strategic Change: Technical, Political and Cultural Dynamics, by Noel Tichy, Copyright ā 1983 by John Wiley & Sons, Inc. Reprinted by permission of John Wiley & Sons.)

Tichy describes the three subsystems (technical, political and cultural) as a rope consisting of three braids. Each braid contains many fibers (management tools). Consequently, if there is a weakness in some of the fibers, it will impact one or more of the braids (subsystems) and subsequently the whole rope.[20]

Another explanation of the function of technical, political, and cultural organization framework functions can be adapted from Senge's view of the functioning of the organizational system. Senge states "The bottom line of systems thinking is leverage—seeing where actions and changes in structures lead to significant, enduring improvements."[21] Consequently, the eight management tools may be viewed as the leverage for the technical, political and cultural subsystems and subsequently, the entire organizational system (figure 2). Examining these eight areas will reveal information about the organization and where changes need to occur.

According to Tichy, organizations never completely resolve the dilemma of these three subsystems. Because environmental changes are constant, organizations are to be dynamic and always undergoing change. This model was developed to provide organizations with a conceptual framework and methodology for examining and implementing change. Therefore, the dynamic organizational model was selected for this case study.

Figure 2: TPC Systems

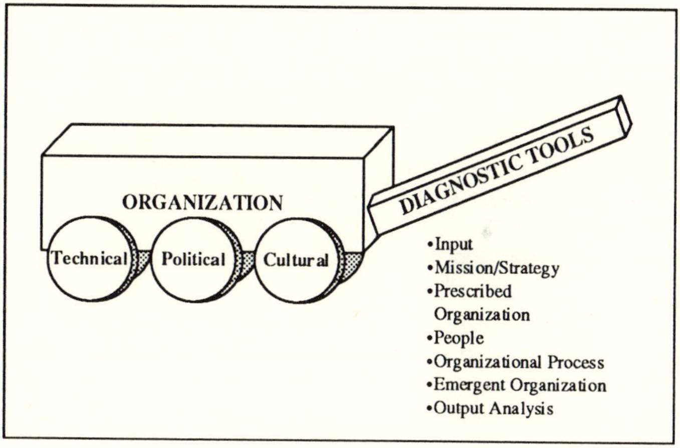

RESEARCH QUESTIONS

The following major research questions were formulated within the three subsystems for this proposed study:

1. How did DTA develop as an African American entrepreneurial firm?
2. What obstacles have the leaders and managers of the firm encountered in the management of the firm?
3. How did the leaders and managers overcome these obstacles?
4. Have there been any identifiable phases of development of the organization in its seventeen years of existence?
5. How did DTA develop a multi-ethnic staff?
6. How has DTA maintained a multi-ethnic staff?

DEFINITIONS

The following definitions were used in the study:

- Entrepreneur—One who searches for change, responds to it, and exploits it as an opportunity. The entrepreneur shifts areas of low productivity and yields to areas of higher productivity, and may start companies.[22]
- Entrepreneurship—Organization started by an entrepreneur and whose central focus is innovation, creativity, and continued growth.
- Ethnicity—The bio-genetic inheritance of an individual.
- Manager—An individual with the title of manager who has the responsibility for maintaining the organization's functioning in an assigned area.
- Officer—One who holds a title of Vice President or Assistant Vice President.
- Organizational life cycle—Organizational changes due to evolution through successively more complex stages of development.
- Owner—One who owns shares in a firm.
- Principal—A senior executive or owner of a firm.

- Prime Consultant—A business that pursues a project directly with the owner. The prime firm, or consultant, contracts directly with the owner. The prime firm also contracts with other firms, or subconsultants, which work under the direct supervision of the prime firm.
- Professional—An individual with a degree in engineering, architecture, marketing, management or business and who performs those related services for the company.
- Project Manager—One who is responsible for managing a project and carries the title of Project Manager or On-Site Coordinator.
- Subconsultant—A firm that contracts with a prime consultant to provide a specific service for a project. The subconsultant is responsible to the prime consultant, not the owner.
- Support Personnel—An individual, under direct supervision of a supervisor, who provides services that assists the organization in its general function (i.e., secretarial services, technician, etc.).
- Threats—Turbulent conditions in the internal or external environment which could affect the existence of an organization.

DELIMITATIONS AND LIMITATIONS OF THE STUDY

Introduction

The implications and recommendations of the proposed study were evaluated in the context of the following delimitations and limitations.

Delimitations

This study was conducted on one firm, Don Todd Associates, Inc. (DTA), and had one interviewer, the researcher. A self-selected representative sample was used. A random sample was not used because it was necessary to include key individuals (i.e. the president, accountant, etc.) in the sample. The proposed study was also delimited to the use of the *Organizational Interview Protocol* as the interview tool.

Limitations

The major limitation of any case study is that it cannot be generalized to the larger population. Researcher bias is possible since the researcher is also a member of DTA and married to the president of the firm.

SIGNIFICANCE OF THE STUDY

Introduction

The significance of the proposed study may be seen from three perspectives: the implication and recommendations of the study to assist DTA in planning its future; contribution to the literature on African American entrepreneurships; and contribution to the Tichy model.

Implications and Recommendations for DTA

The proposed study provided an analysis of DTA's past, present, and future. Information was obtained about the critical elements of DTA's past and how decisions regarding those elements were made. Data regarding current internal and external organizational threats, with possible solutions, was also gathered. The value of the proposed study was the information and insight it provided the DTA leaders and managers regarding DTA trends that led to positive results, as well as the organizational need for future direction. From this analysis, data for a strategic plan emerged that will assist the organization in planning for a successful future.

Contribution to Literature on African American Entrepreneurship

There is a paucity of literature on the growth, development and challenges of African American entrepreneurship. Most of the literature presents biographical sketches of the entrepreneur or highlights the successes of African American-owned companies. This proposed study will benefit the African American community by providing details of an African American firm that has organized and sustained itself over a period of time. In addition, the study will emphasize the challenges an African American firm has faced and how they were overcome. The systematic review and evaluation of DTA will prove a valuable role model to African Americans aspiring to own a business.

Contribution to the Use of the Tichy Model

The Tichy dynamic model has been used to analyze community, educational, and medical facilities, and a family-owned small business. Utilizing the TPC model as the conceptual framework for the analysis of an African American-owned business provides an additional perspective for the use of this model.

NOTES

1. *Engineering News Record*, "Top 100 CM Firms," 21 (June 1993): 33.

2. Timothy Ichniowski, "The Main Men On Public Works," *Engineering News Record* 6 (September 1993): 24.

3. *Engineering News Record*, "Special Report: Forecast '94," 31 (January 1994): 45.

4. William G. Krizan, Harry Bradford, and Susan W. Setzer, "Scent Of Recovery Is In The Air," *Engineering News Record* 31 (January 1994): 73.

5. *Fiscal 1993 Audit Report of Don Todd Associates, Inc.*, January 1994.

6. *Principal's Report*, "Exercising Leadership: California Principals Prepare to Rebound from the Recession," (December 1993): 16.

7. Ibid., p. 14.

8. *Engineering News Record*, "Turner Bites Bullet Now to Improve Profitability and Productivity Ahead," 4 (April 1994): 28–29.

9. Udayan Gupta and Jeanne Saddler, "Financing Prospects for Black Businesses Remain Poor," *The Wall Street Journal* 16 (May 1994): B2.

10. Jeanne Saddler, "Young Risk-Takers Push the Business Envelope," *The Wall Street Journal* 12 (May 1994): B1.

11. Matthew Dorf, "NYC Kills Set-Aside Program," *Set-Aside Alert* 1 (January 1994): 1.

12. Ibid., p. 10.

13. Allison Samuels, "Succession Planning in African-American Businesses," *Upscale* (March 1994): 34–38.

14. Ibid.

15. Gwendolyn Glenn, "Getting Down To Case Studies," *Black Issues In Higher Education* 10 (1993): 26–27.

16. Ibid.

17. John R. Kimberly, "The Life Cycle Analogy and the Study of Organizations," *The Organizational Life Cycle*, J.R. Kimberly and R.H. Miles, eds. (San Francisco: Jossey-Bass, 1980), p. 2.

18.   Robert Quinn and Kim Cameron, "Organizational Life Cycles and Shifting Criteria of Effectiveness: Some Preliminary Evidence," *Management Science* 29 (1983): 33–51.

19.   Noel Tichy, "Managing Strategic Change: Technical, Political, and Cultural Dynamics," *Organizational Assessment and Change*, E. Lawler III and S.E. Seashore, eds. (New York: John Wiley, 1983).

20.   Ibid.

21.   Peter M. Senge, *The Fifth Discipline* (New York: Doubleday/Currency, 1990), p. 114.

22.   Peter F. Drucker, *Innovation and Entrepreneurship: Practice and Principles* (New York: Harper and Row, 1985).

II

Organization of the Literature

MAJOR THEMES OF THE LITERATURE REVIEW

The purpose of this study was to conduct an in-depth analysis of Don Todd Associates, Inc. (DTA) in order to assist the organization in making the necessary changes to secure its future. A review of the literature revealed there are major factors which affect the life cycle of an organization and how it changes to secure its future. In addition, DTA is an organization that is influenced by three unique factors: the firm is an entrepreneurial organization, it is 100% owned by African Americans, and it has a multi-ethnic work force. Consequently, the literature was also reviewed to determine the major factors influencing this African American-owned entrepreneurial firm with a multi-ethnic staff. Four major themes were identified that assisted the focus of this research:

- Organizational life cycles
- Entrepreneurial theory of organizations
- African American entrepreneurial organizations
- Multi-ethnic work force and organizational culture

ORGANIZATIONAL LIFE CYCLES

The life cycle concept of organizations is embedded in the philosophy of change. Organizations change due to a dialectical change process or as a result of the organization's evolution through successively more complex stages of development.[1] Much of the research focuses on the cyclical growth of an organization, similar to one's passage of life. Kimberly states that organizations have a cyclical quality—they are born, grow, and decline and must be renewed or they will disappear.[2] Whetten is one of the few authors to discuss organizational decline.[3] The author indicates that the focus on growth led to the idea that organizational decline is simply failure to follow principles of a growth-mandated paradigm. According to Whetten, this idea is related to the belief that it is primarily small firms that fail. Now that large organizations are failing, decline is viewed more seriously. Decline is now referred to as "retrenchment" and is not always viewed as negative. Whetten urges that decline and retrenchment be studied more carefully. While growth and decline is the law of nature, it may be possible for organizations to continue renewal for a long and effective life. Adizes contends that with "foresightful management" an organization should outlive its key managers.[4]

Lippitt and Schmidt emphasize that an organization goes through predictable stages and will have predictable crises. These authors believe that how the leaders of an organization recognize and respond to these crises will have a serious impact on the organization's continued to growth.[5] An example is the model established by Larry Greiner. Greiner alleges that while organizations evolve, this evolution is due to growth and environmental crises.[6] He maintains that growing organizations move through five stages of development. Each stage ends in a leadership crisis, which influences the next phase and allows management to anticipate and prepare for the next stage. The components of Greiner's model are:

1.   Creativity—The company's emphasis is on creating a product and a market. The Founders are usually technicians or entrepreneurs with no emphasis on management. Communications and structure are informal. Long hours and dedication to the company and/or product are prevalent. The *crisis* occurs when the organization grows and new employees do not have the fervor of the initial group. Customers request larger quantities in shorter time frames. Additional capital is needed, and new financial and accounting control procedures are required.

2. Direction—A period of sustained growth under directive leadership usually follows the first phase. A more formal organization is developed separating technical activities and marketing. Accounting systems for inventory and purchasing are introduced. Incentives, budgets, work standards, titles, and "positions" are adopted, and communication becomes more formal. The leader institutes direction while specialists manage the technical work. *Crisis* occurs when specialists and technical personnel feel more knowledgeable about the market and product needs than the leaders and feel restricted by a cumbersome and centralized hierarchy.

3. Delegation—Responsibility is delegated. Profit centers and bonuses are used to motivate staff. Managers manage the exceptions. Communication from the top is infrequent, usually limited to correspondence, telephone, or brief visits to field locations. *Crisis* of control occurs when top management and leaders become alarmed at a loss of control.

4. Coordination—The organization is consolidated, and decentralized groups are merged into product groups. Formal planning procedures are established and intensely reviewed. Corporate functions are centralized at headquarters while daily operational procedures remain decentralized. New staff are hired to initiate company-wide programs that provide better control of employees and production. *Crisis* occurs because a bureaucratic paper system has evolved. Staff resent the direction from those unfamiliar with local conditions. Procedures seem to take precedence over problem solving and initiative.

5. Collaboration—Interpersonal collaboration and participative management become the key to overcoming the formal control and red tape crisis. Social control and self-discipline take precedence over formal control. The focus is on solving problems quickly, using a team approach. Functional teams are developed, and whenever possible, corporate staff is reduced and reassigned. Key leaders and managers interact frequently with staff in a variety of roles. Staff creativity and innovation is encouraged. Economic rewards are geared to team performance rather than individual performance. *Crisis* is undefined at this time.

The inference is that leaders should recognize that organizations change, identify the current level of organizational functioning, and prepare the organization for an impending change. They should not panic when they recognize change but develop planned strategies that will help the organization through the crisis and facilitate the next phase of evolution.

There are many life cycle models of organizations. Cameron and Quinn[7] combined nine such models. They reviewed the models and their proposed characteristics for each stage of organizational life cycle development. The authors then developed a summary model to integrate the nine models (including Greiner's model). The integration of the nine models yielded four stages of organizational life: entrepreneurial stage, collectivity stage, formalization and control stage, and elaboration of structure stage.

Churchill and Lewis developed another life cycle model from existing models.[8] These authors developed a growth model for small businesses based on the work of Steinmetz and Greiner. The revised model was tested on 110 owners and managers. These businesses had sales ranging from $1 million to $35 million. After going through a small company management program and reading Greiner's article, respondents answered a questionnaire. Respondents were asked "to identify as best they could the phases or stages their companies had passed through to characterize the major changes that took place in each stage and to describe the events that led up to or caused these changes."[9] The authors then categorized the results of 83 of the questionnaires. The comparison of the questionnaire results and the revised model led to further revisions which resulted in the current five stage model:

- Existence—acquiring customers and delivering a product.
- Survival—emphasis on cash flow concerns.
- Success—avoid cash flow drain in prosperous periods; emphasis on *success disengagement* (owner begins to move away from the business activities as the company remains stable) or *success-growth* (owner consolidates the company and obtains the resources for further growth).
- Take-off—focus is on delegation of responsibility and authority and maintaining cash to support growth. If the company does not prosper, it may now retrench into a smaller, stable company.

- Resource Maturity—emphasis is on reserving the entrepreneurial spirit, maintaining flexibility, and becoming a formidable force in the market.

The authors also identified eight key management variables which must be managed differently as the organization progresses through various stages of development. Five of the variables are related to the entrepreneur and determine the mission and culture of the firm. These factors are the owner's personal and business goals, capabilities, management style, and strategic planning abilities. These variables determine the skills and abilities necessary for management, delegation, marketing, innovation, planning and visionary thinking. Churchill and Lewis also designate four key factors that relate to the company. These factors include financial resources, personnel resources, systems resources, and business resources. These factors determine the cash flow, quality and depth of human resources, planning and information systems, customer relations, product distribution, and technology. The authors state that this model could help owners of small businesses analyze current challenges, diagnose current problems, and develop appropriate solutions.

The strength of this model is that it identifies both evolutionary stages and management issues that may be critical to a growing firm. Another strength is that it does not limit the creativity and innovative response of the entrepreneur to a stage of organizational development. However, a question remains regarding biased responses by the participants. The training received prior to completing the questionnaire could have biased their responses. Comparison of trained and untrained groups may have strengthened the reliability of the data.

The evolutionary approach to an organization's life cycle is very descriptive of the stages of development. However, the stage by stage view of an organization is limited. First, it does not view the organization as a social system with an interaction between the roles and expectations of the institution and the people who work for the institution. In addition, the demands of the environment are not considered. Another limitation is that the evolutionary life cycle concept does not account for an organization's unique qualities. It describes gross stages of development rather than the systems or people that make up an organization. Finally, the evolutionary process identifies areas that may need to be resolved, but because it does not describe the interaction of various systems and people, these recommendations are vague.

The open systems model contrasts the cyclical view of organizations with definitive stages. This dynamic view provides a framework for understanding the correlation of an organization's input, output, and environments. The open systems model describes systems and cycles of information, resource input, transformation, and output. The organization is viewed as being interdependent with the system and the environment. An open system is viewed as being dynamic because there is constant change, movement, and energy flow by which the organization sustains itself.[10] Dyer developed an open-systems framework which has three subsystems: social, technical and administrative.[11] His social system focuses on human relations in the organization, including communication and climate. The technical subsystem involves the activities needed to accomplish the tasks or work product of the organization. The administrative subsystem is the formal structure of the organization, including the formal organizational structure, budgets, and reporting relationships. The focus of this framework is to identify the influences of the organization's internal system on its output. The success of the system is dependent on the balance and mutual reinforcement of the subsystems. The strength of this model is that it acknowledges the interaction of the social system and the organization. Examining the balance of these systems is important in the development of an organization. However, this model does not adequately consider the role of the external environment on the system.

Another open systems framework is the Technical, Political and Cultural (TPC) model developed by Noel Tichy.[12] Tichy believes that the constant change and growth of an organization can best be described by observing how the organization responds to uncertainties brought about by internal and external environmental threats, opportunities, organization size, or technological trends. These uncertainties affect one of three subsystems: technical, political or cultural. Because organizations are subject to constant environmental change, and are therefore dynamic, the dilemma of the three subsystems is never completely resolved. This research rests upon this dynamic organizational model.

DTA's unique characteristics determined the choice of model for the analysis. The three most important factors are that DTA is an entrepreneurial organization, African American owned, and has a multi-ethnic staff. What the literature revealed about these three factors is discussed in the following section.

ENTREPRENEURIAL THEORY OF ORGANIZATIONS

What is an entrepreneurial organization, how does it function, and how is it unique from other organizations? No universal answer has been developed. There are entrepreneurial theories and perspectives that derive from the disciplines of economics, sociology, psychology, and organizational theory. When reviewing each perspective there are two observations that become apparent:

- None of the theories or perspectives are complete within themselves because they do not account for each of the other disciplines involved in entrepreneurship.
- All of the theories and perspectives of entrepreneurship are based on the definition and perception of the entrepreneur, which differs with each theory.

The word "entrepreneur" is believed to have been coined by the French economist Jean Baptiste Say around 1821.[13] Say indicates that the entrepreneur shifts resources out of an area of lower productivity into an area of higher productivity and greater yield.[14] There has since been much discussion about the definition of entrepreneur and entrepreneurship. Schumpeter was one of the first Americans to study the entrepreneur. The author described the entrepreneur as an individual whose function was to carry out new combinations of means of production.[15] Schumpeter believes that innovation was the central characteristic of entrepreneurial behavior. Vesper was one of the first authors to describe the entrepreneur as one who could be found working with other individuals in a large organization.[16] Peter Drucker also indicates that while the popular definition of an entrepreneur is an individual who starts one's own business, that notion is a misconception. Not every new small business represents an entrepreneurship.[17] Drucker states that an entrepreneurial business can be small or large but is chiefly characterized by innovation, creativity, and growth. He further states that entrepreneurship "is behavior rather than personality trait and its foundation lies in concept and theory rather than in intuition."[18]

Carland, Hoy, Boulton and Carland also state that "All new ventures are not entrepreneurial in nature. Entrepreneurial firms may begin at any size level, but key on growth over time. Some new small firms may grow, but many will remain small businesses for their organizational lifetimes."[19] Using these definitions, an entrepreneurship can be defined as an organization based on innovation, change and growth.

What is the theory of entrepreneurship? While many researchers discuss "theory" there is no central entrepreneurial theory. Amit, Glosten and Muller believe that the interdisciplinary nature of entrepreneurship precludes the development of a single theory.[20] The authors define entrepreneurs as being "those who are profit-seeking, either working individually or in a corporate setting, and those who are not profit seeking, working in charitable, government and other not-for-profit organizations."[21]

A *theory* can be defined as "an explanation of behavioral or physical events."[22] Amit et al. define an *entrepreneurial theory* as being:

> . . . a verifiable and logically adherent formulation of relationships; or underlying principles that either explain entrepreneurship, predict entrepreneurial activity (e.g., characterize conditions that are likely to lead to new profit opportunities and to the formation of new enterprises), or provided normative guidance (i.e., prescribe the right action in particular circumstances).[23]

Considering these definitions, Amit et al. noted that predicting the profiles of individual entrepreneurs or the success of an entrepreneurship can be difficult. Low and Mac Millan[24] also developed a framework from which a theory could be derived. Their framework emphasizes the interdisciplinary nature of entrepreneurship. Behavior must be explained in the context of social/cultural, networking and personality perspectives. Prediction of behavior includes the discipline of population ecology, while normative theory (prescribing the right action for the right circumstance) involves economic perspectives.

Bygrave and Hofer also support the perception that a challenge to the entrepreneurial field is the development of sound theories.[25] They first indicate that it is necessary to shift the focus from the entrepreneur and the entrepreneurial traits, to the entrepreneurial process. Entrepreneurial research needs to follow the path of management research, which switched the focus from the functions and responsibilities of the manager. "If researchers could develop a model or theory to explain the entrepreneurial processes, they would have the key that unlocks the mystery of entrepreneurship."[26] These authors believe that any theory of entrepreneurship must consider the volitional act of the entrepreneur moving from a position of not having a business to having a business. The theory must be grounded in the social sciences (economics, sociology, political, psychology or anthropology) in order to be holistic and include the multitude of social/cultural variables that underlie the development of the entrepreneur and entrepreneurship. Finally, they also agree that a theory must have predictive power.

A brief review of some of the definitions and theories that are associated with various disciplines will reveal some of their differences and deficiencies.

Economic Perspective

Much of the modern American thought about entrepreneurs and entrepreneurship is based on the early work of Joseph A. Schumpeter. It is with Schumpeter that the emphasis becomes focused on creative response and innovation.[27] He defines creative response as being a response by the economy or an industry that is different from existing strategies. The creative response is "something that is outside of the existing practice."[28] Consequently, he viewed a study of the creative response in business as having the same scope and boundaries as the study of entrepreneurship. He indicates that the very definition and function of an entrepreneur is based on innovation. " ... The entrepreneur and his function are not difficult to conceptualize: the defining characteristic is simply the doing of new things or the doing of things that are already being done in a new way (innovation)."[29] Consequently, the process for achieving results in a capitalist society depends upon the entrepreneurial activities of that society. Schumpeter is also known for his perceptions of entrepreneurial decline. He believed that the importance of the entrepreneurial function will decline over time, akin to the role of the traditional warrior which has declined with the inclusion of modern technology in warfare.

Social/Cultural Perspective

While the economic perspective studies the role and response of the entrepreneur to economic conditions, the social/cultural perspective examines the role of culture and situations in the initiation and development of entrepreneurship. Studies and theories in the social/cultural perspective perform situational analyses that explain the cause of the formation of entrepreneurship. There is a traditional belief that given the right set of circumstances entrepreneurship will automatically develop. As Carroll states, "Implicit in this approach is the belief that the entrepreneur is not only a cause of change but also a product of changing forces operating within a society, that entrepreneurship is not only a scarce resource but a resource which itself is produced by one set of forces rather than another."[30] The research in this area attempts to determine which groups (social, ethnic, cultural, institutional, economic, etc.) generate the most entrepreneurs and why.

One concept that emerged from this perspective is that cultural deviance and social marginality produce entrepreneurial activity. Hagen[31] explained entrepreneurial behavior in terms of the lower status groups seeking to overcome their current situation by means of economic creativity and innovation. He used historical research based on firms in Japan, Colombia, England and Russia. While Glade did not support the theory of "marginality" as the only reason for entrepreneurship development, he did believe that situational analysis is preferable over comparative statistics analysis in developing a theory of entrepreneurial growth.[32] He stated,

At least, therefore, a growth model of entrepreneurship must make allowance for such elements as the fluidity of demand patterns in the domestic market (which is a function, in turn, of income and income distribution trends, the exposure and receptivity of the culture to influences which change tastes, demographic trends, urbanization, etc.), the relation of the locale to actual or potential foreign markets (and supply resources), and the like.[33]

There are other situations that may contribute to one initiating a business. Shapero and Sokol[34] discuss voluntary migrants as having a high rate of entrepreneurial activity. The authors state that when a person leaves one environment for another, for whatever reason, that individual experiences displacement in the new society and environment. The authors speculate that the more an individual is excluded from the new environment, the more likely the individual will create a new venture.

This perspective suggests that entrepreneurship develops as a result of situational and cultural factors. Consequently, this is the perspective that has been used to explain entrepreneurial development among various ethnic groups.[35]

Psychological Perspectives

Both the economic and the social/cultural perspectives are macroanalyses of entrepreneurship. That is, they look at individual response to economic, social and cultural events. However, not all individuals respond the same way to the same environment. The focus of the psychological perspective is to determine what makes an individual initiate and sustain entrepreneurial activity. This is one of the largest bodies of entrepreneurial knowledge and tends to focus on the traits of an entrepreneur. Understanding the personality traits of an entrepreneur is central to the discussion of entrepreneurship, since the existence of an entrepreneurial organization is dependent on the entrepreneur. Timmons refers to the entrepreneur as the driving force in the entrepreneurial process.[36] Consequently, a microanalysis of the individual entrepreneur is appropriate.

McClelland[37] was one of the first to empirically study the entrepreneur. He determined that entrepreneurs had a higher achievement need than business executives. Consequently, McClelland developed the theory that there was a causal link between need for achievement in individuals and the economic growth and decline of nations. It should be noted, however, that McClelland's definition of the entrepreneur was very general and often included persons such as management consultants, salespeople, or officers of a large company. Frey[38] argued that McClelland's theory was empirically invalid and theoretically inadequate.

Organizational Perspective

The organizational perspective of entrepreneurship is centered around the definition of an entrepreneurial organization. Is an entrepreneurial organization one founded by an entrepreneur; and does it remain an entrepreneurial organization as long as it fits certain characteristics? Or is an entrepreneurial organization a stage of organizational development in organizations that are started by entrepreneurs? Or can an entrepreneurial organization be one that has been established for many years, but is based on innovation with one or more separate business ventures as part of its overall organization? Gartner[39] defines entrepreneurship as the creation of new ventures. He further states that entrepreneurship ends with the conclusion of the creation stage. Gartner concurs with Greiner[40] that an organization can live beyond its creation (entrepreneurial) stage and move into other stages, such as growth, maturity, and decline.

Corporate entrepreneurship, or intrapreneurship, as it is sometimes referred to, is the act of performing entrepreneurial functions in an already established organization. Nielsen, Peters and Hirisch defined intrapreneurship:

> ... the development within a large organization of internal markets and relatively small and independent units designed to create, internally test-market and expand improved and/or innovative staff services, technologies or methods within the organization.[41]

The third definition of entrepreneurship as an organization is somewhat inferred from the definition of entrepreneur. Cole clearly describes this position by defining entrepreneurship as:

> . . . the purposeful activity (including an integrated sequence of decision) of an individual or group of individuals, undertaken to initiate, maintain or aggrandize a profit-oriented business unit for the production or distribution of economic goods and services.[42]

As indicated in this brief review, entrepreneurship has been defined by the behavior or the traits of the entrepreneur. The entrepreneurial process has had less focus, but neither the definition of entrepreneur nor the theory behind the entrepreneurial process has been stated in a manner that integrates the various disciplines involved in the entrepreneurial process. It is clear, however, that being an entrepreneur and functioning in an entrepreneurial organization is distinct and different from other managerial activities. To this end, this research analyzed an organization that is entrepreneurial—an organization that is founded by an entrepreneur and whose central focus is innovation, creativity and growth. Consequently, the framework selected for this analysis must be flexible enough to incorporate the entrepreneurial organization.

AFRICAN AMERICAN ENTREPRENEURIAL ORGANIZATIONS

Much of the literature on African American entrepreneurship focuses on the entrepreneur rather than the entrepreneurial organization. The history of African American entrepreneurship dates back to the entry of Africans into America. Initially, Africans entered America as indentured servants.[43, 44] As indentured servants, they worked for a European American until they earned their freedom, after which they obtained jobs or developed their own farms—an entrepreneurial venture.

However, most Africans brought to America were slaves. While this brutal form of human bondage was designed to totally control the individual for the slave owner's personal gain and eliminate all possibilities of freedom, some slaves were motivated to pursue entrepreneurial activities.[45] Moreover, as freed women and men, it became necessary for African Americans to develop businesses to meet their particular needs—hairdressers, neighborhood stores, mortuaries, schools, and restaurants. Other businesses such as lumbermills, photography, and law were also established. Kilar chronicles the struggles of black entrepreneurs in Saginaw, Michigan.[46] He described a community that had enterprising African Americans, including a lumber mill entrepreneur, a photographer (with a studio), and a restauranteur. He also indicated that the European American community tolerated the entrepreneurial growth for only a short time:

> By the turn of the century, the climate of tolerance and acceptance had dissipated, and the enterprising Black man no longer discovered ready avenues leading toward financial prosperity. Nonetheless the nineteenth century Black man should be commended.[47]

Modern day African Americans span many occupations. Venable[48] characterized most Black businesses as confined to the service and trade industries and being marginally successful. He believed that most African American businesses were relegated to businesses in their own neighborhoods, using family members as staff and conducting business with a small percentage of the population. A more recent profile of African American business was completed by Ragsdale, who studied entrepreneurship by profiling the African American entrepreneur in Maricopa, Arizona.[49] He studied twenty-seven minority entrepreneurs in Maricopa County, Arizona (which includes the Phoenix metropolitan area) to determine a profile of African American entrepreneurs. The research focused on the entrepreneurs' history, reasons for going into business, start-up, continuing problems in the business, leadership skills, and types of business. The information was obtained by a structured interview process. Most of these businesses were characterized by the author as being small, and many were "in-home" businesses. However, the profile of the African American businesses (16 of 27 in the study) showed that 42 percent served all people, 29 percent served European Americans, and 29 percent served predominately African Americans. More than 90 percent of the African Americans worked at sites other than their homes. The average number of years in business was 14.6. While this study did not directly address entrepreneurial practices, the following comments were made in conclusion:

> The successful minority entrepreneur is a rare breed who, out of necessity, overcame the odds of competition and survival statistics. The forces that developed a minority entrepreneur were many that were fostered and nurtured by difficult times and circumstances, but the hierarchy of human needs prevailed as a motivating force to press minorities to the pinnacle of success, however small. . . .

> Minorities face a myriad of difficulties when they embark on the trail. Oppression, suppression, and depression are the common roadblocks, but other factors force delays and detours. The lack of adequate financing and business guidance, as well as formal and specialized education, often relegate a minority business to a marginal one. It is next to impossible for a minority enterprise to thrive from the labor and earnings of poor people.

> The advice to the potential minority entrepreneur is:

> - Be committed
> - Be aggressive
> - Be adequately financed
> - Be knowledgeable about competition
> - Be honest
> - Be aware of the level of family support
> - Be knowledgeable about the market
> - Be prepared to cope with adversity[50]

Another study of African American-owned firms concentrated on discovering the strategies that African Americans use to adapt and survive in difficult economic and social circumstances.[51] Ndulue states that the black owners of a construction firm used spatial, internal, and vertical mobility strategies to adapt to changes which contributed to the successful entrepreneurship. It has traditionally been believed that Blacks could not move into certain areas of business, particularly those enterprises requiring heavy capital investment and having a potential for growth and the capacity to serve a more diversified population. According to Ndulue's study, more Blacks are moving into these areas and developing successful businesses. The reasons for failure were the following:

• lack of capital and access to markets,
• poor education and inadequate preparation to compete in these areas,
• lack of social capital essential for successful business operation in a competitive multi-ethnic city,
• racial discrimination and segregation that impose severe constraints on Black entrepreneurial pursuits.[52]

Ndulue interviewed 16 successful black entrepreneurs and did an extended case study of one black entrepreneur who owned a construction company. The results of this study indicated that African Americans in urban settings use a survival strategy to overcome social and economic marginality. This is an example of the social/cultural perspective of entrepreneurship and the assertion that persons in marginal social and economic situations use creative and innovative strategies in order to overcome their personal situations.

A popular source of information about African American entrepreneurship is *Black Enterprise*. Most of these articles focus on the entrepreneur, entrepreneurial traits, and the development of a growing business. The thrust of most articles on entrepreneurship is usually descriptive rather than analytical. Recent articles have emphasized the need to expose young African Americans to black entrepreneurs and the option of business ownership through organized programs such as the Southwest Atlanta Youth Business Organization.[53] One of the more detailed articles in *Black Enterprise* describes the African American entrepreneur, Herman J. Russell of Atlanta.[54] Herman Russell has built a conglomeration of 13 Atlanta-based companies under the umbrella of H.J. Russell & Co. The article focuses on Russell's entrepreneurial behavior dating from his youth, personal problems he has faced, and the general management strategies he used to build his empire.

An article on Donald J. Todd, Founder of Don Todd Associates, also focuses on Todd as the entrepreneur.[55] However, the article does provide a list of recommendations to assist potential entrepreneurs in initiating and starting their own businesses (figure 3).

The literature on African American entrepreneurship is not plentiful. What literature exists, focuses on the entrepreneur as opposed to the organization. Most of the literature is descriptive as opposed to analytical. However, two problems that have surfaced in the literature are acquisition of adequate capital and racism. Some authors believe that black businesses have difficulty providing services to a diverse ethnic community. The framework upon which this study is based must be flexible enough to allow these types of issues to surface and be analyzed.

Figure 3

Don Todd's Entrepreneurial Checklist

- Acquire "hands-on" experience *before* embarking on your own.
- Do not become encumbered with large personal debt.
- Develop some capital to live on while your business is getting started.
- Develop and refine communication skills: writing, speaking and, especially listening skills.
- Build a *relationship* with a banker. Let them know who you are and what you do, and open a business account.
- Utilize the services of a good attorney and CPA whenever needed.
- Make sure you pay all taxes relative to your business in a timely manner.

- Secure all needed kinds of insurance in the right amounts for the company, and build a relationship with the insurance companies.
- *Always* keep track of your bottom line (profit/loss).
- Hire only competent people, as they are an extension of you.
- Focus your business in an area that you know well. Do not become scattered trying to provide too many services or products.
- Have your brochures and written literature done in a professional manner. *First impressions are lasting.*
- Be responsible to your clients - return phone calls promptly; meet commitment dates.
- Be a person of integrity in all your business and personal relationships.

(Source: Todd, 1994, p.23)

MULTI-ETHNIC WORK FORCE

One of the changes that most organizations are facing is an increasingly multi-ethnic labor force. The multi-ethnic work force is usually discussed in the literature as "work force diversity." The emphasis is on equipping corporate America to take advantage of the skills of America's diverse population in order to excel in the global market. Focus is given to developing high performance of quality diverse teams—with an understanding, appreciation, and ability to value and respect different races, ethnic groups, cultures, languages, genders, ages, religions, sexual orientations, physical abilities, and family structures.[56] Consequently, it has become necessary for corporations to "manage diversity" in order for America to continue to prosper.[57] How African American firms with multi-ethnic work forces view and develop their organizations has not been explored in the literature.

Workforce 2000: Work and Workers for the 21st Century has been deemed a landmark book by many corporate executives, awakening them to the fact that the labor force is rapidly changing. The book emphasizes the fact that more than ever, women, people of color, physically challenged individuals, older workers and gays and lesbians are entering the workforce.[58] The change in workforce population has resulted in a change in the values that dominate corporate culture. Projections based on the 1990 census indicate that four out of every five persons employed in the year 2000 will be people of color or women.[59]

The review of the literature indicated that most corporations realize that a changed workforce results in changes within the corporate culture. An example of the impact of diversity on the organizational culture was noted in Rhinehart's study of three ethnic groups of custodians working for the same company. He discovered that three problem areas surfaced. The first area was identified as diversity, or the problem of combining culturally different ways of working. The second problem was identifying truth, or knowing what to believe when the culturally familiar patterns were not available. The third problem area was that of "voice" or having other cultures heard within the dominant organization.[60] This change in corporate culture impacts overall work productivity and effectiveness; therefore, organizations are examining more closely how to best manage the change in corporate culture. Diversity training programs have become a popular solution. Leung noted that of 18 companies interviewed in the Kansas City, Missouri area, 11 had formal diversity training programs, and the others were either actively researching a program or had other methods of promoting diversity in their company.[61] Prior to a discussion on diversity issues, a brief discussion of corporate culture is warranted.

Organizational Culture

Organizational culture is defined as the accepted way people in a specified group think, speak, act, learn, and transmit information from generation to generation. A more specific definition is

> the pattern of basic assumptions that a given group has invented, discovered, or developed in learning to cope with its problems of external adaptation and internal integration, and that have worked well enough to be considered valid, and therefore, to be taught to new members as the correct way to perceive, think, and feel in relation to those problems.[62]

Deal and Kennedy[63] state that the elements of corporate culture consist of the business environment, values, heroes, rites and rituals, and the cultural network. Of these, values are deemed to be the heart of corporate culture. "Values define 'success' in concrete terms for employees—if you do this, you too will be a success and establish standards of achievement within the organization."[64] These authors further state that corporate culture is the key to good management and an effective organization.

> A strong culture is a system of informal rules that spells out how people are to behave most of the time. By knowing what exactly is expected of them, employees will waste little time in deciding how to act in a given situation. . . . A strong culture enables people to feel better about what they do, so they are more likely to work harder.[65]

Schein also supports the concept that corporate culture determines organizational effectiveness. He indicates, in his definition of culture, that organizational culture addresses external adaptation and survival problems as well as internal problems of integration.

Clearly, the more homogeneous the group the stronger the corporate culture. Schein states that "the strength or amount of culture can be defined in terms of (1) the homogeneity and stability of group membership and (2) the length and intensity of shared experiences of the group."[66] If this statement is correct, how then does a corporation manage a heterogenous group with newcomers? How does this diverse group affect the organizational effectiveness of a culture? According to these authors, a heterogenous group with newcomers would produce a weak organizational culture, which in turn, would decrease the organization's effectiveness.

Based on the assumption that homogeneity produces a strong culture, how does the inclusion of persons of differing genders, ethnicities, and cultures affect the corporate culture? Deal and Kennedy addressed this question from the perspective of assimilation:

> Day-to-day life in a company's culture revolves around countless repetitions of unwritten but well-understood rituals. Mostly social in context, one purpose they serve among others is to introduce newcomers to the culture. When the newcomer is different—a woman in a man's world, or a black in a white managerial echelon—no rituals exist to socialize this individual. In the place of comfortable rituals are taboos: "Don't hustle that woman"; or "Blacks are sensitive, so be careful not to hurt their feelings."

> Entering the ritual life of a culture becomes a hurdle women and minorities have to overcome. . . . Membership in a subculture of outsiders affects women and minorities personally and professionally. But just as significantly, it affects overall corporate operations too. A company cannot get the best work from anyone who is an outsider looking in. The economic reasons should be quite apparent.[67]

Corporate Diversity

It appears that the economic component of corporate culture has flourished and moved to the forefront of the corporate culture discussion. Companies are coming to recognize that in order to compete globally and achieve maximum productivity, they must make the best use of a changing workforce, with regard to cultural behaviors. Fernandez[68] discusses the steps that a corporation must take in order to excel in the global market. He emphasizes the American, European, and Japanese markets, stating that the focus needs to be on developing high performance and quality, diverse teams with an understanding and appreciation of, and ability to value and respect different races, ethnic groups, cultures, languages, genders, ages, religions, sexual orientations, physical abilities, and family structures.

Thomas also supported the concept that corporations need to empower the total workforce by managing diversity.[69] He stated that while the traditional approach to managing diversity has been assimilation, the time has come for a new, more effective approach. Assimilation expects the newcomers to accept the burden of trying to "fit• into the existing corporate culture. Thomas believes that assimilation is so widespread that managers and employees have "bought into• the concept, essentially saying to newcomers:

> We have determined in this company that there is a specific culture, and that people who fit a given mold do better than those who do not. As you join us, we're going to hold up a mirror in front of you. In this mirror, you will note that we have sketched the outline of the mold that works here. If you fit, fine, come on in. If you don't, we invite you to allow us to shape you to the appropriate mold. This is for our mutual benefit, as it will help to ensure that you have a productive relationship with the company.[70]

Thomas indicates that forced assimilation produces employees who play it safe in order to fit into the culture, which in turn, produces a lackluster performance in today's competitive environment. In addition, individuals of different ethnic groups, genders, physical abilities, sexual preferences, etc., believe that their cultures, values and beliefs are strengths that should not be compromised by assimilation, but should be included in a manner that strengthens the organization. In order to obtain this goal, Thomas indicates that there are three approaches devised to go beyond assimilation: affirmative action, valuing diversity and managing diversity.

Thomas viewed affirmative action as a temporary form of legal and social action necessary to ensure the creation of a diverse workforce and the upward mobility of those individuals. Valuing diversity is the attitude of an organization which encourages awareness, understanding and respect for diversity within the organization. Managing diversity ensures that the organization's system works well for everyone and requires examination and change of the root culture of the organization to enable the necessary changes to occur. Managing diversity requires mutual adaptation by the organization and the individual.[71]

Another diversity model emphasizes the need to empower people of color. Many persons of color in large, mostly homogeneous corporations may have experienced hostility to the extent that their self-esteem and personal value are greatly diminished.[72] Lyles believes it is unlikely that anyone, including white males, wishes to give up power. Consequently, managers of color must be empowered to present an opposing force in order to break the old stereotypes and behavior patterns.[73] Lyles indicated 13 self-limiting behaviors:

- Silence in the face of discrimination
- Blame the victim of discrimination
- Distancing from other minorities
- Over achievement while underemployed
- Social isolation from non-minorities
- Waiting for later rewards
- "Doing a good job" as sole career strategy
- Over credentialing
- Refusal to hire or promote other minorities
- Conflict avoidance
- Limited aspirations
- Low self-initiation strategy
- Rejection of expertise or authority of other minorities[74]

She also discussed six strategies for "finding a voice" :

- Confronting the reality of racism as an element of organizational life
- Having the moral courage to take unpopular positions
- Authentically responding to microinequities (small acts of racism)
- Developing risk embracing strategies
- Supporting activism and voice by others
- Coalition building with non-minorities[75]

Lyles acknowledged that a thorough, well focused and well funded diversity program is a long term investment for change—10–30 years. In the interim, people of color need a leadership training program to assist in rebuilding courage and confidence, so that each person may act on his or her own behalf and move away "from victimization to activism." The author believes such a training program will assist people of color to be fully empowered to use their skills and creativity.

SUMMARY

A review of the literature revealed that an entrepreneur is defined as an individual whose behavior is centrally characterized by innovation and creativity. This individual may start a business or exhibit these behaviors in the business for which they work. An entrepreneurship, then, is a business characterized by innovation, creativity and growth.

The organizational life cycle was studied using an evolutionary and a dynamic model. The evolutionary model supports the idea that, like human life, an organization evolves by going through various stages. The dynamic organizational model states that the growth of an organization can best be described by observing how the organization responds to uncertainties regarding internal and external environmental threats, opportunities, organization size, or technology. When determining which model to use for the study, three unique factors about DTA were considered: it is an African

American-owned firm; it is an entrepreneurship; and it has a multi-ethnic staff.

The emphasis in the literature on African American entrepreneurship was on the entrepreneur rather than the business. The characteristics of an African American entrepreneur and the individual difficulties encountered in developing a business were well documented. However, the process by which the African American-owned business venture develops, changes, and grows was not well documented. The literature did suggest that black-owned business must cope with racism, difficulty acquiring capital, and difficulty serving diverse ethnic populations.

The literature on entrepreneurship reveals a myriad of definitions and theories rising out of different disciplines. There is no one unifying theory or definition, as entrepreneurship is a multi-dimensional phenomena, and no current theory or definition includes all disciplinary perspectives. Consequently, a definition of entrepreneurship for this study was chosen. An entrepreneurship is defined as an organization that experiences continual growth with innovation and creativity. The innovation and creativity may be in the creation of the product itself or in the way the product is marketed, processed, or promoted. This definition is consistent with the early economic philosophy of Schumpeter.

The focus of the literature on a multi-ethnic workforce is "diversity." Fernandez and Thomas emphasize that American businesses will have to develop, understand, and appreciate diverse quality teams in order to remain competitive in the global arena. Diversity, in this case, refers to the inclusion of different ethnic groups, genders, cultures, ages, religions, sexual orientations, family structures, and physically challenged individuals. There is little known about multi-ethnic staffs in minority-owned firms.

There is a large body of literature on entrepreneurs, entrepreneurship, and organizational change and growth. However, when these topics become further specified by delineating the ethnicity of a business to be African American, the literature becomes very scant. In addition, most multi-ethnic staff issues seem to be a concern of large European American-owned businesses. There is little emphasis on how businesses who have multi-ethnic staffs develop. There is no information about the effects of minority-owned businesses with multi-ethnic staffs on the business arena.

The dynamic model, specifically Tichy's TPC framework, was chosen as the framework for this study. It was believed that this type of model would allow for the discovery of any evolutionary pattern within DTA; permit an exploration of the unique factors about DTA; and provide a study of the technical, cultural, and political subsystems of the organization.

NOTES

1.   Peter Blau, *On the Nature of Organizations* (New York: John Wiley, 1974).

2.   John R. Kimberly and Robert H. Miles, "Social and Behavioral Science Series," *The Organizational Life Cycle*, John R. Kimberly and Robert H. Miles, eds. (San Francisco: Jossey-Bass, 1980).

3.   David A. Whetten, "Organizational Decline: A Neglected Topic in Organizational Science," *Academy of Management Review* 5 (1980): 577–588.

4.   Ichak Adizes, "Organizational Passages—Diagnosing and Treating Lifecycle Problems of an Organization," *Organizational Dynamics* 8 (1979): 3–25.

5.   Gordon Lippitt and Warren Schmidt, "Crises in a Developing Organization," *Harvard Business Review* 45 (1967): 102–112.

6.   Larry E. Greiner, "Evolution and Revolution as Organizations Grow," *Harvard Business Review* 50 (1972): 37–46.

7.   Robert Quinn and Kim Cameron, "Organizational Life Cycles and Shifting Criteria of Effectiveness: Some Preliminary Evidence," *Management Science* 20 (1983): 33–51.

8.   Neil C. Churchill and Virginia L. Lewis, "The Five Stages of Small Business Growth," *Harvard Business Review* 61 (1983): 30–39.

9.   Ibid., p. 44.

10.   Daniel Katz and Robert L. Kahn, *The Social Psychology of Organizations* (New York: John Wiley, 1966).

11.   W. Gibbs Dyer, *Strategies for Managing Change*, (Reading, MA: Addison-Wesley, 1984).

12.   Noel Tichy, "Managing Strategic Change: Technical, Political, and Cultural Dynamics," *Organizational Assessment and Change*, Edward Lawler III and Stanley E. Seashore, eds. (New York: John Wiley, 1983).

13.   Peter F. Drucker, *Innovation and Entrepreneurship: Practice and Principles* (New York: Harper and Row, 1985).

14.   Jean Baptiste Say, *The Production, Distribution and Consumption of Wealth*, French trans. from 4th ed. (Boston: Wells & Lily, 1921).

15.   Joseph A. Schumpeter, *The Theory of Economic Development* (Cambridge, MA: Harvard University Press, 1934).

16.　Karl H. Vesper, *New Venture Strategies* (Englewood Cliffs, NJ: Prentice-Hall, 1980).

17.　Peter F. Drucker, *Innovation and Entrepreneurship: Practice and Principles* (New York: Harper and Row, 1985).

18.　Ibid., p. 26.

19.　James W. Carland, Frank Hoy, William R. Boulton, and Jo Ann C. Carland, "Differentiating Entrepreneurs From Small Business Owners: A Conceptualization," *Academy of Management Review* 9 (1984): 354–359.

20.　Raphael Amit, Lawrence Glosten, and Eitan Muller, "Challenges to Theory Development in Entrepreneurship Research," *Journal of Management Studies* 30 (1993): 815–834.

21.　Ibid., p. 816.

22.　Walter R. Borg and Damien Gall, *Educational Research: An Introduction* (White Plains, NY: Longman, 1989), p. 54.

23.　Ibid., p. 819.

24.　Murray B. Low and Ian C. MacMillan, "Entrepreneurship: Past Research and Future Challenges," *Journal of Management* 14 (1988): 139–161.

25.　William Bygrave and Charles Hofer, "Theorizing About Entrepreneurship," *Entrepreneurship Theory and Practice* (Winter 1991): 13–22.

26.　Ibid., p. 14.

27.　Joseph A. Schumpeter, "Creative Response in Economic History," *The Journal of Economic History VII* (1947): 149–159.

28.　Ibid., p. 150.

29.　Ibid., p. 151.

30.　John J. Carroll, *The Filipino Manufacturing Entrepreneur* (Ithaca, NY: Cornell University Press, 1965), p. 3.

31.　Everett Hagen, *On the Theory of Social Change* (Homewood, IL: Dorsey Press, 1962), pp. 191–198.

32.　William P. Glade, "Approaches to a Theory of Entrepreneurial Formation," *Explorations in Entrepreneurial History* 4 (1967): 245–259.

33.　Ibid., p. 249.

34.　Albert Shapero and Lisa Sokol, "The Social Dimensions of Entrepreneurship," in *Encyclopedia of Entrepreneurship*, Donald L. Sexton, Calvin A. Kent, and Karl Vesper, eds. (Englewood Cliffs, NJ: Prentice-Hall, 1982).

35. Ibid., pp. 80–81.

36. Jeffrey A. Timmons, *New Venture Creation*, 3rd ed. (Homewood, Il: Irwin, 1990).

37. David McClelland, *The Achieving Society* (Princeton, NJ: D. Van Nostrand, 1961).

38. Scott R. Frey, "Need for Achievement, Entrepreneurship, and Economic Growth: A Critique of the McClelland Thesis," *Social Science Journal* 21 (1984): 125–134.

39. William B. Gartner, "'Who is an Entrepreneur?' is the Wrong Question," *Entrepreneurship Theory and Practice* 13 (1989): 47–68.

40. Larry E. Greiner, "Evolution and Revolution as Organizations Grow," *Harvard Business Review* 50 (1972): 37–46.

41. Richard Neilson, Michael Peters, and Robert Hirisch, "Intrapreneurship Strategy for Internal Markets—Corporate, Non-profit and Government Institution Cases," *Strategic Management Journal* 6 (1985): 181.

42. Arthur H. Cole, *Business Enterprise in its Social Setting* (Cambridge, MA: Harvard University Press, 1959), p. 7.

43. Leon Higginbotham, *In the Matter of Color: The Colonial Period* (New York: Oxford University Press, 1978).

44. Edmund Morgan, *American Slavery, American Freedom: Ordeal of Colonial Virginia* (New York: Norton, 1975).

45. John Chika Agboso Ndulue, *Urban Black Adaptation and Successful Entrepreneurship in Chicago: An Extended Case Study of a Black-Owned and Operated Construction Firm*, Ph.D. dissertation (Urbana-Champaign, IL: University of Illinois, 1985), pp. 91–95.

46. J. Q. Kilar, "Black Entrepreneurs in the Michigan Lumber Towns," *Negro History Bulletin* (1983): 52–53.

47. Ibid.

48. Abraham Venable, *Building Black Business* (New York: Crowell, 1972).

49. Lincoln Johnson Ragsdale, *Minority entrepreneurship: Profiling An African-American Entrepreneur*, Ph.D. dissertation (Cincinnati, OH: The Union for Experimenting Colleges and Universities, 1989).

50. Ibid., pp. 59–60.

51. John Chika Agboso Ndulue, *Urban Black Adaptation and Successful Entrepreneurship in Chicago: An Extended Case Study of a Black-Owned and Operated Construction Firm*, Ph.D. dissertation (Urbana-Champaign, IL: University of Illinois, 1985).

52.   Ibid., p. 234.

53.   Adrienne S. Harris, "Hot Kidpreneur Programs," *Black Enterprise* (February 1994): 177-182.

54.   Nathan McCall, "How Herman Russell Built His Business . . . Brick By Brick," *Black Enterprise* (June 1987): 176–184.

55.   Gwendolyn Powell Todd, "The Gift of a Good Example," *Minorities and Women In Business* (May 1993): 22–23.

56.   John P. Fernandez, *The Diversity Advantage*, (Lexington, MA: Lexington Books, 1993).

57.   Roosevelt R. Thomas, Jr., *Beyond Race and Gender: Unleashing the Power of Your Total Workforce by Managing Diversity* (New York: AMACOM, 1991).

58.   William B. Johnston and Arnold Packer, *Workforce 2000: Work and Workers for the Twenty-first Century* (Indianapolis, IN: Hudson Institute, 1987).

59.   Carole Y. Lyles, "People of Color: Finding Voice," *OD Practitioner* (Winter 1993): 11–16.

60.   Milton Duncan Rhinehart, *Cultural Diversity At Work and Its Effect On Organization Communication and Conflict*, Ph.D. dissertation (Boulder, CO: University of Colorado at Boulder, 1994).

61.   Chi-Sun Benjamin Leung, *Diversity Training in the Corporate World of America: A Look at the Heartland of America* (Warrensburg, MO: Central Missouri State University, 1995).

62.   Edgar H. Schein, "Coming to a New Awareness of Organizational Culture," *Sloan Management Review* 25 (1984): 3.

63.   Terrence E. Deal and Allan A. Kennedy, *Corporate Cultures: The Rites and Rituals of Corporate Life* (Reading, MA: Addison-Wesley, 1982).

64.   Ibid., p. 14.

65.   Ibid., pp. 15–16.

66.   Edgar H. Schein, "Coming to a New Awareness of Organizational Culture," *Sloan Management Review* 25 (1984): 7.

67.   Terrence E. Deal and Allan A. Kennedy, *Corporate Cultures: The Rites and Rituals of Corporate Life* (Reading, MA: Addison-Wesley, 1982), p. 78.

68.   John P. Fernandez, *The Diversity Advantage* (Lexington, MA: Lexington Books, 1993).

69.   Roosevelt R. Thomas, Jr., *Beyond Race and Gender: Unleashing the Power of Your Total Workforce by Managing Diversity* (New York: AMACOM, 1991).

70.   Ibid., p. 7.

71.   Ibid., pp. 17–33.

72.   George Davis and Glegg Watson, *Black Life in Corporate America* (Garden City, NY: Doubleday, 1982).

73.   Carole Y. Lyles, "People of Color: Finding Voice," *OD Practitioner* (Winter 1993): 11–16.

74.   Ibid., p. 13.

75.   Ibid., p. 14.

III

The Research Method

METHODOLOGY OVERVIEW

The purpose of this study was to conduct an in-depth analysis of an African American-owned firm with a multi-ethnic staff, Don Todd Associates, Inc. (DTA), using the case study method. The results of the analysis will assist the firm in responding to the current internal and external threats it is facing and add to the paucity of literature on African American entrepreneurship. It is critical that the firm have a thorough analysis of its history and its organizational systems because economic and business markets in the 90's are rapidly changing. Many organizations are folding, or merging in order to survive. While DTA is not floundering, it is facing several internal and external challenges that must be responded to in a way that will continue to strengthen the organization. In addition, the firm has developed a multi-ethnic staff, something most organizations are attempting in order to better respond to both social demands and the global market. How DTA developed and maintained its multi-ethnic staff was crucial to the analysis.

RESEARCH DESIGN

A case study research design was chosen for this proposed study. This approach was appropriate because it provided descriptions, analysis of critical interactions, and explanations of events within the phases of development of the organization. The need for a case study approach stemmed from the need to understand a complex situation:

> In brief, the case study allows an investigation to retain the holistic and meaningful characteristics of real-life events such as individual life cycles, organizational and managerial processes, neighborhood change, international relations, and the maturation of industries.[1]

Yin further stated:

> There are at least four different applications. The most important is to *explain* the causal links in real-life interventions that are too complex for the survey or experimental strategies. A second application is to *describe* the real-life context in which an intervention has occurred. Third, an evaluation can benefit, again in a descriptive mode, from an illustrative case study—even a journalistic account—of the intervention itself. Finally the case study strategy may be use to *explore* those situations in which the intervention being evaluated has no clear, single set of outcomes.[2]

Since this research explained how and why DTA has developed into the entrepreneurial firm it is today, the case study was even more appropriate. According to Yin,[3] the analytical research method of the case study is superior to other qualitative methods in answering the "how" and "why" of events.

POPULATION AND SAMPLE

The population of the study was DTA personnel. The *DTA Employee List* served as the basis for selection of the sample. The sample was stratified according to the following categories: role within the organization (owner, officer, manager, project manager, professional, support); ethnicity; gender; and years with the company. The researcher used a self-selected sample of two people in each role. The researcher interviewed this self-selected sample of

12 people in order to ensure representation from the DTA population. Of the twelve people in the sample, seven were African American (two owners, two vice presidents, one manager, one technical professional and one support person); two Asian Americans (both managers); and three European Americans (two project managers and one support person). Four of the twelve respondents were women (two managers and two support persons). The average length of employment at DTA was 7.8 years, and the median length of employment was 7.55. All respondents had worked for DTA two years or longer.

INSTRUMENTATION

The instrument for this study was the interview protocol. The eight dimensions of Tichy's organizational open systems model were used as the basis for development of the interview protocol. The protocol consisted of twenty-three open-ended questions. It was a semi-structured instrument that contained opening and closing statements, open-ended questions and probes. The use of the probe allowed the researcher to obtain more complete information:

> Researchers in education generally include some highly structured questions in their interview guide, but they will aim primarily toward a semi-structured level, At this level, the interviewer first asks a series of structured questions and then probes more deeply, using open-ended questions in order to obtain more complete data. . . . The semi-structured interview, therefore, has the advantage of being reasonably objective while still permitting a more thorough understanding of there respondents opinions and the reasons behind them than would be possible using the mailed questionnaire.[4]

The interview protocol was based on Tichy's Open Systems Model and was a modification of the questionnaire used in Stacey's study.[5] To reiterate, examination of the eight dimensions of the Open Systems model revealed information about how the technical, political and cultural subsystems of the organization function. The model consisted of the following eight dimensions plus an additional dimension of "future", added by the researcher and the validity panel:

1. Input (history, environment, and organizational resources)—4 items
2. Mission/Strategy Analysis (mission, strategy, goals, and organizational processes)—2 items
3. Task Analysis (basic tasks and how they relate)—1 item
4. Prescribed Organizational Analysis (differentiation and integration of the formal organizational structure)—2 items
5. People Analysis (demographic characteristics, managerial styles, and motivational forces of staff)—1 item
6. Organizational Processes Analysis (communication and decision making)—1 item
7. Emergent Organization (informal organization, coalitions, and cliques)—1 item
8. Output Analysis (organizational effectiveness, goal optimization, and behavioral impacts of the organization)—4 items
9. Future (a section added to assess DTA's future)—4 items

Tichy's model and this type of interview protocol were used to study an educational facility, a non-profit organization, and a small business. Rosen[6] studied the life cycle of a voluntary organization. He examined the organization's history, challenges, and changes. Kimberly[7] used the methodology and interview protocol to examine a medical school, and Quinn and Cameron[8] used it to examine a mental health organization. More recently, Stacey[9] used this methodology to examine the life cycle of a small, entrepreneurial family-run business.

VALIDITY AND RELIABILITY

The face validity of the interview protocol was determined by having three experts examine the questions to ensure that questions assessed what they were alleged to measure. The experts included an African American male entrepreneur who owns an environmental and planning business in San Francisco. In addition, he is a San Francisco Public Utilities Commissioner, Past President of the San Francisco Fire Commission, and Past President of San Francisco Black Chamber of Commerce. The second individual was an African American female and is the Manager of Human Resources in a large multinational corporation, headquartered in San Francisco. She conducts interviews for hiring, for assessment of employee opinions about organizational change, and for task force assignments. The third individual was a European American male who is professor at a college in San Francisco and an organizational development consultant. He has designed and conducted many interviews for firms seeking strategic change and improvements. These individuals reviewed the questionnaire and completed a validation questionnaire. All three experts agreed that the Organizational Analysis Protocol was adequate in length (23 questions), given the scope of this case study. They also agreed that the questions asked what they intended to ask, and no questions were deleted. One question was added to the *Demographic Sheet*, two questions were added to the "Future Section" of the *Interview Questions* and one probe was added. Other modifications were made to ensure clarity.

In order to ensure reliability of the data collected, multiple sources were used. The study used perspectives from the interviewees and DTA documents. The researcher's in-depth knowledge of the organization also assisted in obtaining reliable data. The researcher is the Vice President of Business Development and Administration, and has been an employee of the organization for eight years. Thus, the researcher was able to detect if an interviewee's response was seriously inaccurate.

The researcher interviewed three respondents a second time with an unstructured interview style. Some respondents may respond best to an unstructured interview style. Consequently, using two interview styles ensured that all pertinent perceptions were captured.

DATA COLLECTION

The data for this research was collected by interviews and document analysis. All interviews were conducted individually by the researcher. Each interview was tape recorded, and the researcher took notes. The interviews were transcribed and categorized according to Tichy's Technical, Political, and Cultural model. Information gathered from these two sources allowed the researcher to examine DTA's past, present, and future. In addition, the internal and external environments of the organization were examined. The following documents were examined in this study:

- Financial and audit statements
- Personnel files and records
- DTA handbooks
- Meeting minutes
- Board minutes
- Incorporation papers
- Marketing and business plans
- Vision and mission statements
- Correspondence

DATA ANALYSIS

The findings were developed into emerging themes and analyzed as follows:

- The information was categorized in the three subsystems; technical, political, and cultural. Figure 4 highlights the guidelines for categorization.
- The data was analyzed to respond to the research questions of this study.

    1. How did DTA develop as an African American entrepreneurial firm?
       (Questions #1, 5, 6, 7, 8, 9, 10, 12, 14, 15, 19, & 21)

Figure 4

Managerial Areas	| **Mission & Strategy**	**Tasks**	**Prescribed Network**	**People**	**Processes**	**Emergent Networks**
Technical System	Assessing environmental threats and opportunities Assessing organizational strengths and weaknesses Defining mission and fitting resources to accomplish it	Environmental scanning activities Strategic planning activities	Differentiation: organization of work into roles (production, marketing, etc.) Integration: recombining roles into departments, divisions, regions, etc. Aligning structure to strategy	Selecting or developing technical skills and abilities Matching management style with technical tasks	Fitting people to roles Specifying performance criteria for roles Measuring performance Staffing and development to fill roles (present and future) Developing information and planning systems to support strategy and tasks	Fostering the development of information returns which facilitate task accomplishment
Political System	Who gets to influence the mission and strategy? Managing coalitional behavior around strategic decisions	Lobbying and influencing external constituencies Internal governance structure Coalitional activities to influence decisions	Distribution of power across the role structure Balancing power across groups of roles (e.g., sales vs. marketing, production vs. R&D, etc.)	Utilizing political skills Matching political needs and operating with organizational opportunities	Managing succession politics (who gets ahead, how do they get ahead) Decision and administration of reward system (who gets what and how) Managing the appraisal (who is appraised by whom and how) Managing the politics of information control and the planning process	Management of emergent influence networks, coalitions, and cliques
Cultural System	Managing influence of values and philosophy on mission and strategy Developing culture aligned with mission and strategy	Use of symbolic events to reinforce culture Role modeling by key people Clarifying and defining values	Developing managerial style aligned with technical and political structure Development of subcultures to support roles (production culture, R&D culture, etc.) Integration of subcultures to create company culture	Utilizing cultural leadership skills Matching values of people with organization culture	Selection of people to build or reinforce culture Development (socialization) to mold organization culture Management of rewards to shape and reinforce the culture Management of information and planning systems to shape and reinforce the culture	Fostering friendship and affective networks, coalitions and cliques to shape and reinforce the culture

Managerial Tools (column group heading spanning Mission & Strategy through Emergent Networks)

(Source: Tichy, 1983, p. 119. *Managing Strategic Change: Technical, Political and Cultural Dynamics,* by Noel Tichy, Copyright © 1983 by John Wiley & Sons, Inc. Reprinted by permission of John Wiley & Sons.)

2. What obstacles have the leaders and managers of the firm incurred in the management of the firm?
   (Questions #3, 4, 5, 6, 7, 8, 9, 12, 13, 14, 16 & 20)
3. How did the leaders and managers overcome these obstacles?
   (Questions #3, 4, 5, 6, 7, 8, 9, 14, 16,)
4. Have there been any identifiable phases of development of the organization in its seventeen year history?
   (Questions #9, 10, 12, 14, 15, 17, 18, 20, 21, 22 & 23)
5. How did DTA develop a multi-ethnic staff?
   (Questions #11, 15, & 17)
6. How has DTA maintained a multi-ethnic staff?
   (Questions #2, 11, 19)

- The data was also analyzed to determine if DTA developed through specific phases and utilized certain systems for problem solving. This information was useful in determining future decision making and problem solving techniques appropriate for this organization.[10]
- There were several intervening variables in this study that were examined. Whether the respondents differed in their answers to the interviews relative to their professional level within the organization (owner, officer, manager, project manager, technical staff or support personnel) was examined. Response by ethnicity was compared as well.
- The data collected was analyzed and formalized into recommendations for the organization.

NOTES

1. Robert K. Yin, *Case Study Research* (Newbury Park, CA: Sage, 1989), p. 14.

2. Ibid., p. 25.

3. Ibid.

4. Walter R. Borg and Meredith Damien Gall, *Educational Research: An Introduction* (White Plains, NY: Longman, 1989), p. 452.

5. Michael John Stacey, *The Life Cycle Of A Small Family-Run Entrepreneurial Organization: A Case Analysis Of Change and Growth*, Ph.D. dissertation (Amherst, MA: University of Massachusetts, 1991).

6. Michael J. Rosen, *The Life Cycle Development of a Voluntary Organization: A Case Analysis of Uncertainty and Change*, Ph.D. dissertation (Amherst, MA: University of Massachusetts, 1986).

7. John Kimberly, "Issues in the Creation of Organizations: Initiation, Innovation and Institutionalization," *Academy of Management* 22 (1979): 437–457.

8. Robert E. Quinn and Kim S. Cameron, "Organizational Life Cycles and Shifting Criteria of Effectiveness: Some Preliminary Evidence," *Management Science* 29 (1983): 33–51.

9. Michael John Stacey, *The Life Cycle of a Small Family-Run Entrepreneurial Organization: A Case Analysis of Change and Growth*, Ph.D. dissertation (Amherst, MA: University of Massachusetts, 1991).

10. Noel Tichy, "Managing Strategic Change: Technical, Political, and Cultural Dynamics," *Organizational Assessment and Change*, Edward Lawler III and Stanley E. Seashore, eds. (New York: John Wiley, 1983).

IV

Results of the Study

DATA ORGANIZATION

The purpose of this research was to conduct an in-depth case study of an African American-owned firm, Don Todd Associates, Inc. (DTA). The findings of the study are presented in the eight components of the open systems model and analyzed in the three subsystems of the technical, political, and cultural framework developed by Noel Tichy (TPC Framework). The interview questions were based on the components of this open systems model. The components were:

- Input (history, environment and resources)
- Mission/Strategy/Objectives
- Tasks
- Prescribed Organizational Structure (formal)
- People
- Organizational Processes
- Emergent Networks (informal)
- Output
- Future (added by the researcher)

The findings were analyzed using the TPC Framework. The *technical subsystem* consists of the social, financial, and technical resources. Within the subsystem, the following issues are analyzed: opportunities and threats presented by the external environment, strengths and weaknesses of the organization, organizational processes, and how tasks and organizational roles are defined. Problems in this subsystem are solved by goal setting, strategy formulation, organizational design, and the design of management systems.

The *political subsystem* is concerned with allocation of power and resources, who determines the use of resources, and how problems will be resolved. The uses of the organization and who reaps the rewards are also determined.

Finally, the *cultural subsystem* determines what values are held by what people. Beliefs, values, objectives, and interpretations hold organizations together. If there are divergent beliefs, problems will arise which must be resolved in order for the organization to survive.

The emerging themes from the respondents are included. The data is also presented in response to the study's research questions:

1. How did DTA develop as an African American-owned entrepreneurial firm?
2. What obstacles have the leaders and managers of the firm faced in the management of the firm?
3. How did the leaders overcome these obstacles?
4. Have there been any identifiable phases of development in the firm's seventeen year history?
5. How did DTA develop a multi-ethnic firm?
6. How has DTA maintained a multi-ethnic staff?

Additionally, the data is presented in emergent themes within the following areas:

- The data has been analyzed to determine if DTA has developed through specific phases and utilized certain systems for problems solving. This information will be useful in determining future decision making and problem solving techniques appropriate to this organization.[1]
- There are several intervening variables in this study that have been examined. Whether the respondents differ in their answers to the interviews relative to their professional level within the organization (owner, officer, manager, project manager, technical staff or support personnel) was examined. Response by ethnicity was compared as well.

• The data collected was analyzed and formalized into recommendations for the organization.

TECHNICAL, POLITICAL, AND CULTURAL FRAMEWORK AND COMPONENTS

Input

History. In 1977 Donald J. Todd, a civil engineer and construction manager, learned of a business opportunity in San Francisco for a minority-owned construction management firm. He formed his own company, Don Todd Associates, Inc., which was incorporated in the State of New Jersey on October 11, 1977, and subsequently selected as a subconsultant on the $1.6 billion San Francisco Clean Water project. DTA relocated to San Francisco in November, 1977. At that time, Todd owned 51 percent of the company and a venture capitalist owned 49 percent. By 1983, Mr. Todd had purchased his partner's shares, and in 1984 he acquired another minority partner, Daniel Anderson. Mr. Todd then became 70 percent owner, Mr. Anderson became the 30 percent owner, and the firm became 100 percent minority owned. This is the current status of the firm ownership. Mr. Anderson remains in charge of the east coast operation, which is managed from the Cherry Hill, New Jersey office.

Mr. Todd and Mr. Anderson have been friends since 1970 when Mr. Todd was a Vice President at Parametric, Inc., and Mr. Anderson was an engineer at the same firm. Parametric was also a minority-owned construction management firm. Since Mr. Todd worked in the New Jersey, New York, and Pennsylvania areas for over ten years, he had many contacts in the construction management industry. In 1979, when opportunities arose to pursue projects in New Jersey, he hired Mr. Anderson. Mr. Anderson became a partner in the firm in 1984.

Initially, DTA performed work as a subconsultant to large prime firms. Most public works projects were very large and required the capabilities and resources of large firms. However, the affirmative action requirements of the seventies and eighties required these firms to give a minimum percentage of the work to minority businesses. This was easily accomplished, since prime firms generally subcontracted work that they did not have the expertise or resources for within their own companies. Subcontracting to minority or women-owned firms ensured that the large prime firms met affirmative action goals.

In order to qualify as a minority firm, most governmental agencies required the firm to have 51 percent ownership by a minority individual *and* be economically disadvantaged with a dollar limit on gross revenue. The latter requirement varies among agencies. In 1989, DTA began to surpass the dollar limitations established for qualification as a disadvantaged minority, and the firm was decertified as a disadvantaged minority firm by various agencies. Consequently, DTA began to compete for work with the large European American-owned firms. DTA could no longer be considered a minority-owned firm for the purpose of affirmative action goals. Firms that used DTA as a subconsultant, the firms with whom DTA had spent years developing relationships, were now DTA's competitors. Many of these firms did not continue to use DTA's services even though they considered DTA's work of the highest caliber.

Environment. In the early sixties, government agencies began to realize that they were building large projects, but were not necessarily obtaining the best results for the money spent. In order to ensure the quality and timeliness of the work, they began to hire engineering consultants who were knowledgeable in design and construction to monitor the work of contractors and act as the owners' representative. This resulted in quality, timely and cost effective work. Thus, the construction management industry began. Many construction companies developed construction management divisions. A few independent, professional construction management firms also developed. These firms indicated that because they did not perform construction or design, they could maintain a more independent perspective of those processes. Since most of the projects were very large, it was difficult for small firms, particularly small, minority firms, to break into the industry.

In 1977 many city, county, and federal agencies had affirmative action programs requiring that minority firms be given a minimum percentage of each professional services contract. This requirement created by the federal government, afforded DTA the opportunity to obtain its first contract. DTA provided program management planning services for the San Francisco Clean Water project. While these affirmative action programs were in force, DTA was able to network with large European American-owned prime organizations and obtain work as subconsultant on large public works projects. Over the years, government, city, and federal agencies have decreased or eliminated affirmative action goals. Consequently, agencies and large prime firms were less motivated to include minority firms on their projects. Most respondents believed that while the economy has fluctuated and fewer jobs have been available, it is the affirmative action requirement that has most influenced the opportunities available for DTA. Respondents also believed that most prime firms and agencies must be externally stimulated by requirements in order to give work to minority firms, and that removal of the requirement resulted in less work being awarded to minority and women-owned firms.

An overwhelming majority of the respondents identified racism as the major obstacle to DTA's success. Racism was described as the predetermined perception that African American and other minority firms are inexperienced, unqualified and second rate companies. Consequently, clients and large European American-owned firms were less willing to give work to minority-owned firms. This overgeneralized and false perception is fed by public acceptance of negative stereotypes regarding African Americans. Consequently, as DTA has performed well and grown, respondents have been questioned as to whether or not the firm is really minority owned or is a front—a firm actually managed and controlled by European Americans but with majority ownership by minorities to take advantage of affirmative action goals. The respondents felt that many times larger firms and governmental agencies do not initially take DTA, or its President, seriously. Other respondents described racism as a preference for one's own group to the exclusion of other groups. In this case, European Americans were described as preferring other European Americans to the exclusion of African American and non-European ethnic groups. Often the exclusion of other groups is fueled by negative, stereotypical perceptions about one group. The "ol' boy network" is at work—people with power socialize together, choose those similar to themselves, and exclude others.

Most respondents believed that DTA will never overcome racism. One respondent described the situation: "They own the mountain, and we have managed to reach the mountain and climb it; however, it is doubtful that we'll ever get to the top but we *can* get close to it." Another respondent described being black as similar to breathing: "The climate is restrictive, so everyday you go out there and they put obstacles in your way, and you fight a battle every day, perhaps a little harder or a little less, but you fight every day, just so you can breathe." Personal biases against African Americans will always remain and need to be dealt with on an individual basis.

Another word frequently used to describe obstacles the environment presents to DTA is the "stigma of being a minority-owned firm". Respondents explained that generally, in the construction industry, "minority" means being able to do only a limited amount of work, and being able to work only as a subconsultant under the supervision of a large, white consultant firm. Consequently, when someone is informed that DTA is a minority-owned firm, this "stigma" becomes an obstacle.

An example of the situation the respondents were describing is cited from a client satisfaction survey developed by a staff task force and conducted in 1994:

> The task force was concerned as to how to ask a question about clients only using DTA as a minority firm. Although they knew this was true of many firms (because they have stopped using us now that they cannot gain points for using us as a disadvantaged firm), they decided the question was too politically sensitive and did not include it. However, one client clearly saw DTA as a minority firm, only to be used when a minority firm was needed. All of that respondent's answers centered around DTA being a small, minority firm with limited capacity.[2]

Organizational Resources. The company started with a venture capitalist investment in the company as a minority partner. By 1983, the venture capitalist was paid off and the firm subsequently became wholly owned by Mr. Todd and Mr. Anderson. In 1987, the firm qualified under the U.S. Small Business Administration (SBA)–8(a) program. However, during eight years in the program, the firm has never had an SBA guaranteed loan, and obtained only one SBA contract. All finances have come from the firm's revenues and line of credit obtained from a local bank. Cash flow has never been a problem.

The major resources for DTA have been people and computer equipment. The firm primarily hires engineers and architects who use their management skills and computer technology to get their jobs done. Once DTA obtains a project, it is dependent on its people to do the job correctly and provide the service to the client. Consequently, obtaining the project is a major focus of the firm.

Mission/Strategy/Objectives

The mission of the organization has been to provide excellent construction management services while maintaining a profit. Survival, growth and quality have been the key elements of the mission. This concept has been the core of the mission since its inception. Most respondents describe the mission as one that was communicated, not only verbally but by the action of the owners. While the mission was not written, it was clear to the respondents. A task force consisting of staff members from the east and west coast developed the written mission and vision statements in 1993 (figure 5).

Figure 5

Mission Statement DTA	Vision Statement
DTA's mission is to provide excellent cost-effective project and construction management services to the Public and Private sectors nationwide.	Don Todd Associates, Inc., a multicultural business entity will:
As an extension of the Client, we are committed to completing our projects on-time and within budget while consistently maintaining the highest standard of quality.	Be known as an enterprise that provides high quality Project and Construction Management Services nationwide;
DTA provides clients with a highly qualified professional and multicultural workforce that is committed to "owning" the project with a professional investment in the outcome.	Continue the diversification of personnel, project experience, revenue, locations, and market; Function as a team of skilled flexible and knowledgeable experts who represent our Clients' interest and help them obtain the best facility or infrastructure available with current technology;
We will continue to operate our company as a profitable, high quality firm that provides excellent professional services.	Provide opportunities and training to challenge and enable personnel to perform at the peak of their abilities; and Operate the company on a profitable basis while being responsible to the surrounding communities.
	1993

There was no official strategy developed to accomplish the mission. Initially, in 1977–1985, the firm was seeking whatever jobs were available in construction management. The firm did not pursue work outside of the construction management arena. Scheduling and inspection were the construction management services most popularly used. DTA's primary focus was to obtain work as a subconsultant. The firm experienced such rapid growth that one respondent described it as "a pot boiling over." In 1987, seeking to develop a niche, the firm began to actively pursue projects that were profitable, were a "fit" for the company and staff, and would expand the company's portfolio. Since 1990, the firm has been pursuing projects more selectively. Firm background and experience, staff capability, and role as prime or association is assessed. Except for a marketing plan written in 1994 for the Western Region, there has been no formal planning document. Respondents were aware of consistent marketing strategies to package DTA services meet changing client needs.

The goals of the firm have been to make a profit, to maintain ethnic diversity, and to keep the clients happy. This has not changed since 1977. Some respondents (east coast) felt that from 1979–1990 the goal was to be #1, or a major force in the industry. However, they believe that experience has taught that there are problems associated with such a high level of performance. West coast respondents felt that the goal was not quick growth, but to be a force in the industry.

Tasks

The firm has always performed services that fall within the category of project/construction management. These services include cost estimating and cost control, scheduling, inspection, on-site coordination, project management, program management, document control, value analysis and value engineering, contract administration, claims prevention, and change order analysis and negotiation. A firm can provide all or any of these services based on what the owner needs and can afford. In 1977, the firm's first project required the development of a management plan for all the projects in the San Francisco Clean Water Program. Other projects acquired by the firm also involved scheduling services. In 1978, the services expanded to include construction inspection services, and in 1981 the services included estimating, value engineering, claims analysis, and constructibility reviews. DTA's first project as a prime was in 1985 for the Central Contra Costa Transit Authority's Administration and Maintenance Building. Currently, DTA is a full service project/construction management firm that provides all services mentioned as a prime, or in association with other firms.

The construction management tasks are performed by engineers and a few architects who have been trained or have experience managing construction projects or performing individual services. An engineer may be trained in civil or mechanical engineering but also have experience providing cost estimating in the civil or mechanical aspects of a project. Other staff include marketing, accounting, clerical support, and administrative personnel.

Construction management services are interrelated. Staff are often capable of performing more than one service (i.e., cost estimator may also provide scheduling, constructibility review, and value engineering services). Some services may be performed independently; however, when a project is being managed by DTA, the success of the overall project is dependent upon quality performance in each area. Some areas need information from another area in order to complete the task. The level of interdependence of services is dependent on the project. In order to complete a construction management project, the estimator must correctly estimate the cost, the scheduler must accurately plan and schedule the project, and the project manager must integrate the results and manage the project accordingly. Administration, marketing, and technical services are also interdependent. Marketing becomes acquainted with the client, determines the client needs and presents available DTA services. Marketing then introduces the appropriate technical personnel to the client. If the project is awarded to DTA, the technical professionals perform the work and continue to look for new opportunities with that client. Consequently, new work and repeat work will be dependent upon the technical professionals. The work of both the technical and marketing professionals are dependent upon administration services. Teamwork and interdependence is the key to successful DTA services.

The types of services and the methods by which they are performed has remained unchanged. What has changed has been the technology with which the services are carried out. In 1977, scheduling was performed manually and with the assistance of the McDonnell Douglas Scheduling System, for which DTA paid computer time. Currently, DTA has engineers who have personal computers equipped with scheduling, cost estimating, word processing, and data base software. The computer capability has more than doubled the work capacity of each engineer and increased the staff's accuracy. DTA has maintained state-of-the-art computer equipment, networking, and software. DTA has the capability to design custom systems for the client or to use whatever software system the client prefers.

Prescribed Organizational Structure

Most of the respondents were not aware of the presence of organizational charts. They recall that initially there were three people in the firm—the president, one engineer and one secretary. In 1979, the staff began to expand. In 1981, Daniel Anderson was named a vice president and made a partner and senior vice president in 1984. In 1985 three vice presidents were appointed, and there are currently six vice presidents. While there are managers in the organization, no one delineated the roles in the organization, nor was the responsibility of the vice presidents clear. The clearest responsibility of the vice presidents was to supervise multiple projects. The two owners of the firm stated that there were organizational charts, a current version of which is shown in figure 6. The respondents did indicate that as the company has grown, the two owners have delegated more responsibility to the vice presidents and the project managers.

Most respondents recall the first policy and procedures manual as being produced in 1987 . Currently, DTA has an office manager and administrator responsible for developing and managing the policies and procedures. However, documents show that DTA had a Policy and Procedure Manual as early as 1979. The manual was revised and distributed in 1987. Project manuals have been developed as needed.

Figure 6

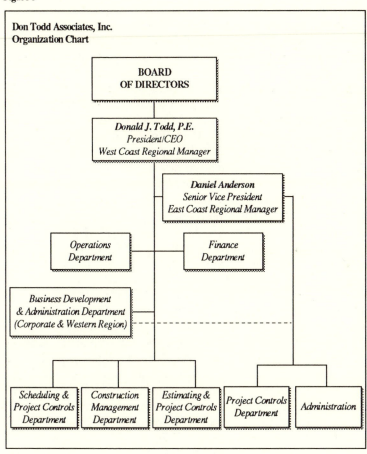

Don Todd Associates, Inc.
Organization Chart

BOARD OF DIRECTORS

Donald J. Todd, P.E.
President/CEO
West Coast Regional Manager

Daniel Anderson
Senior Vice President
East Coast Regional Manager

Operations Department

Finance Department

Business Development & Administration Department (Corporate & Western Region)

Scheduling & Project Controls Department

Construction Management Department

Estimating & Project Controls Department

Project Controls Department

Administration

The lines of authority were clearly delineated as proceeding from Mr. Todd to Mr. Anderson, and then to the vice presidents (four on the west coast and two on the east coast). Some east coast respondents believed that employees tended to go directly to the President or Senior Vice President with their concerns instead of the vice presidents. Below the level of vice president, there was no differentiation of authority.

The line of authority over budgets clearly went to the president, Donald Todd. Lines of authority over personnel, policies, and procedures were not clear. There were no formal or standing committees.

Most respondents indicated that, with the exception of the appointment of vice presidents, the prescribed organization has not changed. The focus for most individuals is on their work, and they do not concern themselves with the formal organization.

The first formal structural change was the addition of Dan Anderson as a vice president to develop an east coast office. The second structural change was the termination of the relationship with the venture capitalist and the addition of Mr. Anderson as a partner. The third structural change was the addition of three vice presidents, Mr. Hattin, Mr. Willis, and Mr. Petreas, with Mr. Anderson being promoted to Senior Vice President. The fourth structural change was the addition of specific departments—marketing and administration in 1986, and estimating and accounting in 1987. The marketing and administration department develops and implements marketing strategies, develops and maintains client relations, develops the corporate image, conducts business development activities, develops and implements administrative and employee policies and procedures, and manages office administration. The marketing section of this department has grown from one individual in 1986 to five and one half employees. Administration has five employees.

The accounting department is responsible for invoices, payroll, payables and receivables, responding to audits, and coordination with an outside CPA consulting firm. The accounting department has grown form one person in 1987 to two people in 1991.

The third formal department was the addition of the cost estimating unit to the west coast office in 1987, based on the perception of a need in the local market. Cost estimating is a service provided as part of construction management services. Design firms also use cost estimating services to estimate the cost of their designs. While the unit continues to provide services during construction, it primarily provides services to designers and owners. In 1989, Alex McClendon was hired to upgrade and develop this department to meet the perceived market need. The department has grown from two full time employees, to twelve full-time cost estimating employees and three interns. The department's responsibilities have expanded to include other traditional construction management services, with ten employees, a total of 22 employees.

Subsequently, the scheduling and construction support department expanded from supporting one project to developing a San Francisco Bay Area service region with five employees.

The east coast has projects with supervision provided by a senior vice president and a vice president and other designated personnel, but no formal departments have been established.

People

DTA has always been a minority-owned company and became 100 percent minority owned in 1983. The first two employees (Donald Todd and a secretary) were African American, and the hiring of two European Americans in 1978 produced a multi-ethnic organization. DTA hired staff as the need arose by demand of the newly acquired projects, rather than retaining staff and seeking projects to meet staff specifications. The goal has always been to hire the best person for the project; the individual with the right project experience and the right educational background. While there is a goal of maintaining a significant number of minority employees, there have not been any special recruiting attempts or a designated number of minority employees set. Through classified advertising in the paper and employee referral, DTA has employed highly skilled people who are ethnically diverse.

The ethnic makeup varies according to office. One respondent indicated that the ethnic makeup seems to be a reflection of the ethnic makeup of the geographic area in which the office or project is located. For example, the San Francisco office has more Asian Americans and other ethnicities while the east coast offices seem to be primarily African American and European American in their population. This is reflective of their respective geographic areas. Respondents indicated that while DTA has always been ethnically diverse, the proportions of diversity simply increased as the company grew. Figure 7 reflects the current ethnic break down of DTA staff.

Figure 7

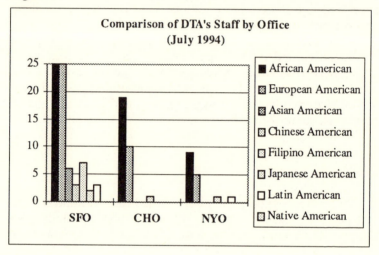

Some individuals responded to an advertisement not knowing that DTA was an African American-owned firm. Others came to the organization knowing that it was an African American-owned firm and wanted to work for a such a firm. Most of these individuals either knew someone who worked for DTA or had known of the firm through its reputation. Respondents felt that it was very positive for DTA to have and present a multi-ethnic staff to clients.

Respondents describe the management style as being participative and collaborative from its early years. However, in most major decisions, Donald Todd received the input of staff and made the final decision. As the company grew, the managerial process became more structured, and vice presidents were delegated the responsibility of managing several projects, and project managers were given responsibility for managing their individual projects. Instead of informal meetings to discuss issues and make decisions, there are now regular staff meetings. On the east coast, respondents felt that the Senior Vice President, Mr. Anderson, has become more autocratic in his style of management in conjunction with employing participative and collaborative forms of management. They see this as a necessary response to the initially loosely structured operation. The laxness was not appropriate as the firm grew. One individual said, "We were a family affair, now we are a business."

The respondents indicated that they have remained at DTA because the firm has been able to offer them a variety of project types and job opportunities. They indicated that the firm does excellent work, the people working for the firm are easy to get along with, and there is no "politicking" in the firm. One person stated, "I can be just be myself at work." Another said, "What matters most is how well I do my job and how happy the clients are with my work." Another said, "Being mean to people and politicking is not tolerated here. We do our work and help each other out."

Organizational Processes Analysis

Communication. In 1977, with only five people in a small office, communication was very informal. Communication was simple, open and spontaneous. As new personnel were added, the communication continued to be informal, with symbolic behavior and verbal communication being the primary modes of communication. Around 1985, more memos were produced, and more people were being assigned to different job sites. As of 1991, communication became more formal with scheduled meetings and memos.

The west coast staff stated that in the past they had more communication with Donald Todd but now go through the vice presidents, and have less face to face interaction with him. Respondents from both coasts, especially those off-site, indicated that they would like more information about company activities and plans. Employee newsletters are produced sporadically.

Decision Making. Most of the respondents viewed Donald Todd as having been the major decision maker from the organization's inception. Other respondents believe Mr. Todd and Mr. Anderson are the major decision makers. The respondents report that the Mr. Todd and Mr. Anderson are flexible and receive input from employees regarding ideas and issues. However, Mr. Todd and Mr. Anderson make the final decisions on major items such as budgets.

Reward System. DTA promotes people as the need presents itself. Promotions are based on hard work, the opinion of the supervisor, job performance, verbal and written skills, technical competence, and interest in the company's advancement in the market place. This has been true throughout the existence of the company.

Conflict Management. In the early years, there were too few people to experience conflict. Disagreements were minor and tended to be worked out through talking with each other. Currently, some conflicts are handled among the employees, but if not resolved, progress to the manager or the appropriate vice president. If the problem is not solved at that level, it is handled by the President.

Most problems on the project site are handled at the site. Often the problem disappears because the projects are for a fixed duration. Some problems are simply repressed, with the hope that they will go away.

Emergent Organization

The respondents stated that they enjoy working at DTA because people exhibit genuine concern for each other and they feel free to be themselves. Ethnic clusters do not bother the respondents. People in the same ethnic group may go out to lunch together, or people of different ethnicities may go out together. A west coast employee observed a situation where two Filipino American engineers were discussing a project in Tagalog. When a Latin American engineer came into their work area, the discussion continued in Spanish. Finally, an African American went into the area to discuss the plans, and the discussion switched to English. People do not care what language is spoken as long as it is appropriate for the work situation.

However, on the east coast, there is some tension between African Americans and European Americans. Some of the European Americans are perceived as believing they can run the company better than African Americans. This tension on the east coast has increased as more European Americans have been added to the staff.

Cliques, or groups of two or more people working together to influence the organization, were not viewed as existing now or in the past. It is believed strong work performance influences the organization. There is not an old and new guard.

Output Analysis

The organization has been very effective in reaching its goals. The goals of the organization have been profitability, growth, maintenance of a diverse staff, and client satisfaction. Formal measures of these goals were not developed or documented until recently. A review of the organization's revenues from 1977 indicates the organization's growth and profitability pattern (figure 8). Long term contracts (four years or more) sustained the firm and provided stability. Long term contracts began in 1977 with the San Francisco Clean Water Program (1977 to present). Other long term contracts were the Camden County Municipal Utility Authority Program, Camden, New Jersey (1986–1994); Bay Area Rapid Transit

Figure 8

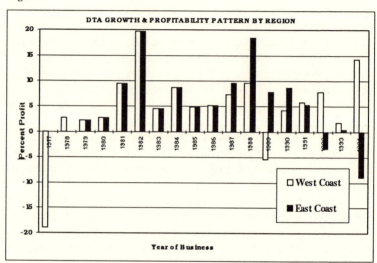

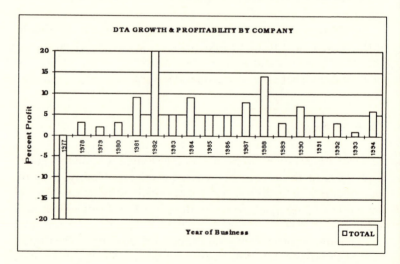

Program, Oakland, California (1989 to present); and the Secaucus Transit Program, Secaucus, New Jersey (1993–1998 est.).

With the exception of the first years of existence, the organization has demonstrated continued growth. The east and west coasts support each other when one is having a less profitable year. The west coast experienced a decline in profitability in 1989, and the east coast has experienced a decline in profitability for the past three years (figure 8).

The records regarding ethnic breakdown indicate that, with the exception of the first two years when the firm was 100 percent African American, the firm has maintained a multi-ethnic staff.

An indication that the firm has a very good reputation among clients and construction management firms is the continued growth and the repeat business the firm receives. A company-wide client satisfaction survey was conducted by the marketing department in July of 1994. The results were:

> DTA appears to be well regarded by the clients interviewed. The services and staff are perceived to be of the very highest quality. Most of the respondents qualified their negative experiences because they did not want the interviewer to think that the negative behavior described was typical. Rather, it was the exception. The fact that the average client knew DTA for 4.75 years speaks to the good service that DTA is providing. Repeat business is a very positive and desirable commodity in a business. While the survey gave a glowing report of DTA, there is room for improvement.[3]

- Most respondents did not identify with a "department" of DTA, but rather an individual. This could lead to problems when that individual leaves or could contribute to the 'small ' image that was perceived by one respondent.
- The respondents did not seem to know all of the services that DTA provided. They were familiar with the service being provided them at the time. This is a limitation that could be affecting DTA's growth and expansion of repeat business.
- There is a desire, on the part of clients, to see more of upper management. The clients that expressed this desire are already seeing DTA Vice Presidents on a regular basis. The clients

indicated that there was nothing wrong, but it was a 'comfort thing'. They would like to see Donald Todd and Daniel Anderson around.

- There are some quality issues that need to be checked: typing errors in the text of one or two reports; invoice adjustments; overwhelming clients with paperwork; and misunderstanding the scope of work. The latter concern was judged to be the fault of the client as well as DTA. DTA management needs to take a more serious look at how these errors occur.

- The task force was concerned as to how to ask a question about clients only using DTA as a minority firm. Although they knew this was true of many firms (because they have stopped using us now that they cannot gain points for us as disadvantaged firm), they decided the question was too politically sensitive and did not include it. However, one client clearly saw DTA as a minority firm, only to be used when a minority firm was needed. All of that respondent's answers centered around DTA being a small, minority firm with limited capacity.

- There was one respondent who seemed to have a less than positive experience with DTA. The respondent was concerned about DTA staff aligning their priorities with the owners, a staff member being unapproachable, and DTA increasing the pay of an individual without approval. This is a large client and the DTA staff work for several different people. This is the same client who found a staff person at DTA to have an "abrasive" personality but the respondent would not change the staff person or would not change the person's personality. However, the respondent did feel that the abrasive personality sometimes made the staff person unapproachable. How to create a balance in both of these situations needs to be discussed.

- When an owner has known DTA and its services and then DTA comes to work on a project through another firm (i.e. as a cost estimator for an engineering firm), a conflict can arise. Because the owner knows DTA's capabilities, requests may be made of DTA that the actual client either may not agree with or does not wish to pay for because it is out of the agreed upon scope of work between the engineering firm and DTA. Yet, DTA feels compelled to please the owner, because of other contracts and repeat work it receives from the owner. This is another situation requiring delicate balance.

- Fees have been a continuing problem at DTA; however, the clients were not alarmed about it. The issue is that DTA has high-quality personnel who must be adequately compensated in order to be retained. We also have personnel who have been with the firm for as long as 16 years. The long-term employee salaries continue to escalate. The costs, of course, are passed onto the client. The issue is: How do we continue to employ high-quality people and bill the costs?

DTA has convened two task forces (one on each coast) which are responding to the issues resulting from this survey.

Future

Future Market. The future of the market for DTA is dependent on the design and construction industry. The responses were divided into two categories—the future market looks good and the future market looks diluted.

Some respondents believed the future market will be good since the economy is showing a slight increase in construction. It is believed that there will always be large construction projects in order to maintain America's infrastructure. DTA has developed experience in all major areas of construction—transportation, municipal, water/wastewater, education, health care, and correctional facilities. These areas are viewed as growth markets. Therefore, these respondents believe there will always be a market for DTA to provide construction management services.

Other respondents felt some concern about the market, as many agencies are developing their own construction management departments. However, these respondents believed that the agencies will quickly find it is not cost effective to maintain their own construction management departments. As a result, there will be claims brought against those agencies, especially since a small department cannot adequately manage large projects. Strengthening the DTA claims department may be lucrative during the anticipated temporary downturn.

The market may also be diluted by construction management services provided by architects and general contractors as their own businesses decline. A possible solution to this dilution resides in "our staff getting to know the client before the project is even developed, so the client will already have confidence in us. We'll have to show the client we can work within their guidelines and can work with their staff members. This situation is going to present a bigger challenge to our marketing team."

Design-build was another concern. Some clients are beginning to utilize design-build—a designer and a contractor work together as a team to produce a project. This type of arrangement restricts the involvement of a construction manager, and supposedly reduces costs. DTA may need to get involved in the design-build process, perhaps by reviewing documents, schedules or estimates for the owner.

Future Challenges. The major challenge seen by respondents is the fact that DTA must compete with the large, European American-owned firm. "Everything we do is going to have to be clearer, sharper and brighter so we can continue to grow." Another member said, "DTA would like to be judged on the quality of work it does, and not be pre-judged when they see that we are African American owned, with a diverse staff. That will always be the major challenge". In order to meet this challenge, one individual said, "I don't think we have to change that or worry about meeting the challenge. I think that it is so ingrained in society anyway, that you just do what you are supposed to do and I think things will usually prove themselves out."

Another challenge is staying competitive. Work availability tends to go in cycles. DTA must remain competitive in order to grow. "Knowing the clients, demonstrating the firm's capabilities and experience, and solving problems quickly and well should help us remain competitive." DTA may also need to consider expanding geographically.

Staffing was seen as another challenge for the future. Clients not only require the company to have the right experience, but also require the proposed project manager to have the right experience and to be the "right fit" for the project. They may want the project manager to have had some of that experience with DTA. Developing resources and insight in hiring people before DTA gets the projects, as well as preparing its current staff for future work, will definitely be a challenge for DTA.

A few respondents mentioned the challenge of planning for succession. No plans have been made for the succession of the Founder and principal owner. One respondent said, "If Don retires, the company will lose its leadership. He is the company."

Modifications Needed to Meet the Challenges. The following were suggestions for improvement:

- Improved communication throughout the organization would result in better job performance and employee satisfaction. Employees who are on job sites often feel cut off from the mainstream. In general, employees may not know the goals of the organization and how they fit into these goals. Some employees may only work with DTA on a specific project. When that project is about to end, there should be more communication with the employee regarding the future with DTA.
- Record keeping needs to be organized, resulting in the ability to obtain information quickly. Currently, any information a project manager or manager needs regarding company staffing, finances, or insurance must be compiled, creating an unnecessary wait. Pertinent corporate information should be readily accessible.
- Employees and vice presidents need more training in order to maintain current knowledge. This would also help DTA become more competitive when recruiting new talent.
- Written manuals for project management and job descriptions should be developed so new employees can be clearer about their role and the expectations of the company.
- Finding the key people that the organization needs.
- The President felt there was a need to review the salary structure. DTA has maintained staff for such a long period of time that the salaries are quite high. This could interfere with DTA's ability to afford new staff or resources.
- Develop a core of middle managers who can operate the company.
- Increase networking with clients and potential clients.

There were some employees who felt that DTA did not need to make any major changes but rather should continue doing what it is doing. The firm needs to stay competitive by providing excellent services and surpassing client needs and expectations. One respondent stated,

> I think it should be stressed that the firm is terribly unique. The more I am out there, the more I learn that there aren't that many firms that are doing what we do, not only in CM, but period. We produce a good product, we are consistent, and we have managed to be apolitical, which theoretically should be the kiss of death, but it's not for DTA. We have continued to be ethical, which is very unusual. I would say those combined qualities make us very unique.

Analysis of Subsystems

Technical

There were very prominent emerging themes in the three subsystems of DTA. In the technical subsystem, it was clear that the opportunities and threats presented by the external environment have been the driving force to which the organization has responded throughout its history. DTA was founded as a response to an opportunity and a need in the construction industry. As the need for minority construction management firms grew, DTA marshaled its forces to meet the demand. It accomplished this feat by hiring highly qualified people when the company had won projects. The company hired people that would be an excellent match for the particular project, again meeting a need and responding to opportunities. In order to remain competitive in the industry, DTA has not only developed outstanding staff, but it has maintained state-of-the-art computer equipment. Now that DTA no longer qualifies with most agencies as a disadvantaged minority, the firm is meeting the need of the client without using the strategy of an affirmative action program. This means acquiring projects as a prime consultant and assuming the leadership role in managing projects. The main obstacle DTA encountered in this transition is one that they have historically faced—the firms and agencies who hire construction managers often equate a minority-owned firm with the inability to lead and manage projects. Their view of minority firms is that they must be subordinate and managed by European Americans. DTA responded to this obstacle by demonstrating its capabilities and maintaining goals of excellence in service to clients in individual and collective performance. DTA also developed appropriate contacts within the industry. The firm has convinced individual clients of its capabilities, and received repeat work from those clients. Gradually the company has gained a reputation for excellence, and the company has continued to grow. While experience, work of the highest quality, and longevity have created credibility, the staff believes it must constantly prove itself each time it encounters a potential new client. One respondent described DTA's situation as similar to that of a boxer, "If you move from the lightweight class to the heavyweight class, you put on an extra ten pounds and can stay in the ring longer, but you never stop being a boxer, you are still in the ring."

The strength of the firm is its management of finances, technical competence, and growth. While the firm has experienced a recent decline in profits, it has maintained a profit throughout the life of the organization. This can be partially attributed to the fact that, while not formalized until recently, DTA has had very clear mission and goals since its inception. The mission has been to provide excellent construction management services and to become a force in the industry. The goals have been to maintain a profit, a multi-ethnic staff, and satisfied clients. It was made clear to each person who worked with DTA that these were the things they were working for. This was reinforced by the behavior of the leaders and rewards to the employees. The respondents believed that the reward system was based on their performance. The strategies to meet the goals were less clear. They ranged from "taking whatever people threw at us" in the late seventies, to "making each project we pursue an investment for our future in some way" in the nineties. Exactly what the strategies were and how they changed over the years was not clear from the available data.

Structure at DTA has not been emphasized and has been used primarily to meet the need of managing growth. The structure and the management has supported entrepreneurial attitudes and interdependent work relationships.

It is not the lack of formal structure that has become DTA's weakness as much as the lack of communication and clear distribution of decision making authority. The organization has grown in number and in geographic location. Therefore, more information must be distributed and made available to employees in various locations. The authority of vice presidents and managers also needs to be made clearer and more consistent between coasts. Staff and vice presidents give input on issues, but it is clear that the major decisions are made by the two owners. This probably results in fewer conflicts because the major decisions are made by a respected owner. Schein indicates that first generation firms are heavily influenced by their Founders, giving the organization its character and biases. Such character and biases are usually easily accepted by the first generation employees because they are so close to the Founders. As new employees and managers are brought on board who do not have the commitment or viewpoint of the Founders, conflicts are more prone to arise.[4] DTA may be on the brink of experiencing this phenomena as it brings on new managers or has a leadership transition.

Cultural

The cultural subsystem is the second most influential subsystem. It has developed and remained stable in this organization. Most individuals seem to enjoy a high degree of job satisfaction. This is due to the fact that the firm has been able to offer them consistent employment, with a variety of project types and challenges. The employees have aligned themselves with the mission and goals of the organization. The owners value individual work performance, and allow people to work independently and interdependently. The staff can be themselves and make a contribution to a growing and successful minority-owned business. While the individuals may bring different cultural and ethnic perspectives, they are able to unify their perspectives and work toward the common goals and values of the organization. These goals include multi-ethnic staff, excellence in performance, excellent people, treating all people fairly, meeting client needs, high level of professionalism, and financial solvency.

People were brought into the organization to meet a need within the organization, or an external need such as a project. An example of an internal need was in 1987 when the finances became too complex and time consuming for the President to handle, requiring the hiring of an accountant.

The main criteria for hiring is finding the best person for the job. The company has not had special programs to attract minorities. The company has maintained a high degree of ethnic diversity since its initial year. Ethnic clusters are seen within the organization, but not cliques and old guard/new guard groups. The old guard/new guard groupings are probably avoided because most of the staff are on project sites, and therefore longtime DTA employees are not around each other to form cliques. Clusters of people from the same ethnic group can be seen, which does not seem to annoy other individuals working in DTA since the groups do not maintain a mutual exclusivity and are organized on a friendship basis. The overriding concern is individual and group work performance. While there is harmony among all ethnic groups on the west coast, there is some tension between African Americans and European Americans on the east coast. The differences in the ethnic make-up could be a contributing factor. On the west coast, there is a variety of ethnic groups, while on the east coast, staff is comprised of mostly European and African Americans.

Political

The political subsystem was the least involved and emphasized in DTA. From its inception, all major decisions have been made by the Founder and owners. These two individuals apparently work exceptionally well together, as there was no report or documentation indicating discord between the two. Some responsibility to manage projects is given to vice presidents and project managers, but the authority level is somewhat unclear.

Until recently, Donald Todd and Daniel Anderson set the mission and goals of the organization. In 1992, a task force was organized to develop a formal mission and vision for the organization. This was ultimately sanctioned by the president and senior vice president. The marketing department developed its own strategies and marketing plan, in conjunction with the technical professionals, and presented it to the president and senior vice president for approval.

Who gets what, and how management succession will be handled is not at all clear. Promotions are given based on the person's performance and success with clients. However, how it will be determined who replaces whom in what position, or who will ultimately succeed the president has not been documented or discussed with vice presidents. Several respondents indicated concern in this area as they believe that Donald Todd is their leader and the person who creates success for the firm. This is consistent with the role of the Founder in an organization as described by Schein.[5]

FOLLOW-UP SESSIONS

In order to assure complete and accurate information, three follow-up interviews were conducted. In addition, the results of the survey were fed back to five employees to obtain their response to the interview results.

The three employees interviewed in individual follow-up sessions were one Asian American female manager, one Asian American male technical engineer, and one European American project manager. These individuals were selected because they had the shortest interview times. The interviews were informal and unstructured. The interviews did not reveal any new information. The three respondents gave the same responses they gave during the formal interview. Their positions did not change.

When asked what they thought of the interview process, each stated that the interviews were very thorough and, as one respondent said, "very bottom line, not superficial". One individual felt there was redundancy in the questionnaire. All three of them said there were areas in the questionnaire that they were not knowledgeable about because they were not involved in those areas.

The group follow-up confirmed that the results of the questionnaire accurately reflected their perceptions of the firm. They supported the suggestion that DTA expand its claims department. They suggested that DTA could become more involved initially by developing a dispute resolution board.

RESEARCH QUESTIONS

1. *How Did DTA Develop as an African American Firm?*

DTA was founded by an African American, Donald J. Todd. He is a registered engineer who founded the company in response to a need and opportunity provided by the City and County of San Francisco through its Clean Water program. The City was required to fulfill federally mandated affirmative action goals by giving a minimum percentage to minority firms. Mr. Todd continued to develop the firm by pursuing projects and hiring the appropriate staff to meet the needs of the client and the needs of the organization. The goals of the organization have been to make a profit, maintain a multi-ethnic staff, and to maintain a high level of client satisfaction. Excellence in work performance is consistently emphasized. Mr. Todd believes in leadership by example.

DTA has grown from five persons to a staff of 125. It has six vice presidents and three persons with the title of manager. The structure has remained loose and flexible. Structure has been developed as the function of the organization has dictated.

2. *What Obstacles Have the Leaders and Managers of the Firm Incurred in the Management of the Firm?*

The respondents have indicated only one major obstacle that this firm has incurred. This obstacle is the belief of firms, agencies and clients that, as a minority-owned firm, DTA does not perform quality work, is not a stable firm, and may be a "front" organization. The respondents often referred to this as racism by groups and individuals who believe the negative stereotypes proliferated about minorities, and African Americans in particular.

3. *How Did the Leaders Overcome These Obstacles?*

The respondents do not believe that DTA has or will ever overcome this obstacle. DTA has proven its quality work, reliability, ethical behavior, and client responsiveness. However, the respondents believe that the firm will have to prove these qualities repeatedly to new individuals, agencies, and firms.

4. What Have Been the Identifiable Phases of Development?

Based on the data, there are three identifiable phases of development:

- Start-up and existence phase—1977–1982. This is the period when DTA was establishing itself as a business, obtaining more than its initial project. The firm performed only as a sub-consultant to larger firms, fulfilling affirmative action goals. Communication was loose and informal. Company goals were expressed verbally and through the leaders' behavior. Management was participative and collaborative and led by Donald Todd.
- Perpetuation and growth phase—1983–1989. During this period, DTA began to experience rapid growth. One of the main strategies was to take advantage of its MBE status, and whenever possible, acquire projects fulfilling MBE goals as a subconsultant and a prime. DTA also started developing alliances with other firms to form associations and joint ventures to pursue projects. The management began to develop through the appointment of vice presidents, the evolution of specific departments, and the development of projects in broader geographical areas.
- Proficiency and growth phase—1990 to present. In this phase DTA is developing as a competitor in the prime arena. It has developed a certain level of proficiency and credibility which has resulted in the firm's success. It no longer fulfills affirmative action goals and has been winning projects independently and making appropriate liaisons with other firms for joint venture or association relationships to pursue projects. Communication is more formal with memos and regular scheduled meetings. More responsibilities are delegated, but major decisions still rest with the president and senior vice president.

5. *How Did DTA Develop a Multi-Ethnic Staff?*

A multi-ethnic staff has always been a goal of DTA. The goal has been realized by hiring the most qualified individual for a particular project. This strategy resulted in the natural development of a multi-ethnic staff.

6. *How has DTA Maintained a Multi-Ethnic Staff?*

Most respondents indicated that they have remained at DTA because the firm has been able to offer them a variety of jobs that maintains their interest. They also stated that the firm's climate allows them to be themselves, and emphasizes and rewards excellent work performance.

PHASE DEVELOPMENT

DTA has developed in three phases, with growth as the primary area of focus. The three phases seem to be start-up and existence, perpetuation with growth, and proficiency with growth. Initially, the firm was challenged to establish itself and acquire enough clients to ensure that it could remain in business. An additional challenge was to develop obtainable mission and goals. In this phase, from 1977–1982, DTA acquired a long term contract which supported the firm while it pursued other work. This is considered the *start-up and existence phase.*

After it was determined that DTA could exist and successfully acquire contracts, the firm began to move into a *perpetuation and growth phase* (1983–89). The challenge was to consistently renew itself, acquire contracts, increase staff and technology, and manage the technical, professional, and financial growth in a manner that supported the DTA goals and mission and would ensure the company's survival. The firm began to acquire as many projects as possible and several long term contracts. One strategy was to take advantage of the affirmative action laws, which allowed DTA as a minority firm to be a subconsultant to other firms. The firm developed contacts, networked, hired high quality staff, and developed good client relations during this time. There was a steady, but high growth rate from 1981–1988. Finances were stabilized with a good cash flow and profit. Goals were continually met.

The third phase is the *proficiency and growth phase* (1990–present). The challenge was to become successful and develop a high level of proficiency in all areas that would continue the organization's growth. In order to do this, the firm had to develop organized, quality service and marketing programs that would allow them to compete independently of affirmative action program strategies. This was also the time to begin to meet the goal of being a force in the construction management industry. The firm has taken off, developed, and utilized a strong cash flow to support its growth and development. The entrepreneurial emphasis has been maintained, and DTA was ranked by the Engineering News Record in 1990 as #67 in the Top 100 CM Firms, and is currently ranked as #58.[6,7]

It appears that the firm is still in the proficiency and growth stage while moving into the *maturity and growth phase*. DTA has moved beyond maintaining existence and survival and is currently experiencing success and self-perpetuation. The next challenge: Is the organization mature enough to survive its current environmental challenges *and* survive reorganization based on succession? If it does so, it will be a mature organization. If it does not transition into this phase, the firm may have to retrench and organize as a smaller firm. This phase will be a test of the firm's entrepreneurial and management strength. Figure 9 highlights the firm's evolution by phases.

The phases of DTA's development most closely parallel the five stages of entrepreneurial development developed by Lewis and Churchill.[8] This model encompasses five stages of organizational growth:

- Existence—acquiring enough customers and delivering a product.
- Survival—emphasis on cash flow concerns.
- Success—avoid cash flow drain in prosperous periods; emphasis on *success disengagement* (owner begins to move away from the business activities as the company remains stable) *or*

Figure 9: DTA Evolution by Phases

	Start-up & Existence 1977-1982	Perpetuation & Growth 1983-1989	Proficiency & Growth 1990-1994	Maturity & Growth Future Questions
Chal-lenge	Become organized as a business & determine whether it can remain operating	Develop firm growth with positive cash flow; obtain repeat business; develop management system to support growth	Develop efficient & proficient services; firm credibility; become competitive on a prime level	Survive environmental challenges, globalization of work, succession of leadership & difficulty of acquiring & maintaining quality staff
Mission Strategy & Goals	Informal; provide excellent CM services; subconsultants as MBE; and hire the best qualified person Goals: Profitable, satisfied client and multi-ethnic staff	Informal; provide excellent CM services; sub as MBE; prime & joint venture; take all projects; and hire best qualified person Goals: Profitable, satisfied client and multi-ethnic staff	Written mission and vision statements; pursue projects as a prime or joint venture in selected markets; choose profitable projects, and hire best qualified person Goals: Profitable, satisfied client and multi-ethnic staff	Will mission, vision, strategy and goals remain the same?
Tasks	Program management, scheduling, inspection, estimating, value engineering, claims, constructibility review	All previous services plus full CM as prime; estimating services for architectural firms, expanded to other geographical areas	All previous services, expansion of CM & estimating services; development of internal Q.A.	Will it be necessary to emphasize one task more than others? Add new tasks? Better quality?
Pre-scribed Network	Informal; east coast employee hired; Donald Todd sole leader with east coast employee (Dan Anderson) becoming V.P.	DTA became 100% minority owned. Dan Anderson became partner and Senior V.P. in charge of east coast. Five VPs appointed; east coast office develops; accounting, marketing and estimating departments established	Officers delegated more responsibility; organization more formal	Will there be a succession, if so what is the plan? Will managers & VPs be more developed and given more authority?
People	Multi-ethnic; engineers & support staff; 2 to 18 employees 800% growth	Multi-ethnic; engineers, architects, technical, support, accounting and marketing 18 to 75 employees 317% growth	Multi-ethnic; engineers, architects, technical, support, accounting, 75 to 120 employees 60% growth	With emphasis on diversity in large institutions, will this stifle DTA's goal? How will DTA get most qualified individuals as a prime?
Organi-zational Process	Informal; personal; verbal communication; behavior observation	Still informal but some meetings; DTA handbook distributed; some memos; verbal communication and behavior observation	Regularly scheduled meetings; more memos	Will DTA improve communication & other processes?
Emer-gent Network	Close; family-like Friendly; supportive	Clusters; no cliques; more structured Friendly, supportive	Regularly scheduled meetings; more memos	Will DTA improve communication & other processes?
Finances	$21,736 - $799,705 = 3579% growth	$858,161 - $4,452,623 = 418% growth	$6,359,399 - $10,516,529 = 65% growth. Became one of Top 100 CM Firms in U.S. by revenue	Will there be growth, stabilization or decline?

success-growth (owner consolidates the company and obtains the resources for further growth).

- Take-off—delegation and maintenance of cash to support growth is the emphasis. If the company does not prosper, this is the time it may retrench into a smaller, stable company.
- Resource Maturity—reserve the entrepreneurial spirit, maintain flexibility, and become a formidable force in the market.

The stages of existence, survival and resource maturity are analogous to DTA's start-up and existence, perpetuation and growth and maturity phases. DTA's proficiency and growth stage seems to be a combination of the success and take-off phases.

INTERVENING VARIABLES

The amount of detailed data presented by an individual seemed to be influenced by the level of the person in the organization. If the person was a vice president, the individual knew more about mission, goals, decision making and planning. With one exception, persons who were in other roles tended to know only about the work they were doing or to speculate on their answers. The one exception was a female manager in marketing who had as much information as the vice presidents. There was no difference with respect to gender, but it should be noted that no female Vice Presidents were included in the sample. The other difference was job location. Those persons located on project sites away from the home office consistently expressed a concern that less information was available to them than individuals located in one of the home offices.

The information obtained from individuals did not appear to vary by any specific ethnic group. Ethnic groups included in the study were African American (seven individuals), Asian American (two individuals), and European American (three individuals). When asked "What are the major obstacles that the leaders and managers of the firm have encountered in managing DTA?" all but two individuals indicated that racism, or the stigma of being a minority-owned firm, was the major obstacle that DTA had to manage. Of the two who stated differently, one was an Asian

American accounting manager who stated that, because all she saw was money steadily coming in, there was no obstacle. The other person was a European American male who said he knew of no obstacles, having only been with the firm two years. When asked "Why do you remain at DTA?" all respondents had the same answer: variety of project assignments, enjoyment working with the people, and freedom to concentrate on their work. When asked how they came to work at DTA, with the exception of the owner and one African American employee, all other African Americans(5), one Asian American and one European American knew DTA was an African American-owned firm when they came to work. The others simply responded to a blind advertisement.

RECOMMENDATIONS

1. First, DTA should examine the positive things it has done and should continue to do:

    -   DTA has defined its services and remained focused on being a construction management firm. It has not attempted to branch out into other service areas which may require additional resources, new markets, and different networking. It has been innovative and creative in the way it presents it focused market niche.
    -   DTA has maintained high quality work performance and personal excellence standards.
    -   The firm has continued to hire employees according to educational ability, experience, and the need of the organization. The goal to maintain an ethnically diverse staff has always been emphasized.
    -   DTA has encouraged individual and collective entrepreneurship.
    -   The firm has created an environment where all people feel they can work, be themselves, and are valued.
    -   The firm has maintained a flexible structure which supports the needs of management rather than dictates the needs of management.

- DTA has been able to offer its staff a variety of projects which created a desire to remain with the company.
- A strong emphasis on client satisfaction and client relations has resulted in repeat business.
- The firm's leaders and owners have maintained a high degree of involvement in the company and have been available to the staff. Additionally, the owners have modeled their values through their behavior and what they pay attention to. Consequently, goal messages have been clear if informal.
- Promotions and recognitions are believed to be based on job performance and client satisfaction.

These are elements of business that DTA needs to maintain.

2. As a growing organization that is geographically diverse, DTA needs to employ a consistent means of communicating with employees. This may be through written updates, job site visits, or town meetings. While too much structure is not desirable, the organization does need to better communicate responsibility in the organization, the organization's mission and goals, and share information about what different departments are doing.

3. Since one of the major goals of the organization is to be profitable, the reasons for the profit loss by the west coast in 1989 and the east coast in 1992 should be examined. While neither of these losses impacted the firm to the extent that there was a corporate loss, it came close in 1992 and 1993. While the revenue has been positive, there has been a great deal of fluctuation, which bears examination. The firm should also examine the impact of long term contracts on the financial picture. For example, the San Francisco office has a long term contract with Bay Area Rapid Transit which may be coming to an end soon. How will the loss of 20+ employees be compensated for or affect the financial picture of the firm? Has there been a pattern established in the past?

4. In order to remain competitive, DTA will need to consider how it will respond to a market that is being diluted with a proliferation of construction management firms, owner construction management, and the design-build concept. Will it take a proactive step in developing a stronger claims

resolution section or a staff experienced with management of design-build projects?

5. Also, in order to remain competitive, DTA will need to consider how to develop and expand its staff. The firm has invested heavily in maintaining its staff. How can it further develop the current staff to meet its future needs, and how will it acquire new staff? While it has acquired new staff in the past, there is no available program for staff development.

6. The review of documents revealed that as DTA has grown, the firm has become involved in more litigation. The financial impact of litigation and the need for prevention programs must be evaluated.

7. Finally, DTA must begin to develop a plan for succession. The staff has become accustomed to, and dependent upon, Mr. Todd's leadership style and decision making capabilities. The east coast employees have become accustomed to Mr. Anderson, but the west coast employees do not know him well. In addition, strong and clear management roles have not been developed throughout various levels of the organization. All major decisions are made by Mr. Todd or Mr. Todd and Mr. Anderson. Respect for other leaders in the organization may be questionable due to the heavy influence of the owners. Consequently, if the firm were to change hands, the firm may experience a serious level of discord that could threaten its existence.

NOTES

1.   Noel Tichy, "Managing Strategic Change: Technical, Political, and Cultural Dynamics, Organizational Assessment and Change," Edward Lawler III and Stanley E. Seashore, eds. (New York: John Wiley, 1983).

2.   Gwendolyn Powell Todd, *DTA Client Satisfaction Survey* (San Francisco: Don Todd Associates, 1994).

3.   Ibid.

4.   Edgar H. Schein, "The Role of the Founder in the Creation of Organizational Culture," *Organizational Dynamics* (Summer 1983): 13–28.

5.   Ibid.

6.   *Engineering News Record*, "Top 100 CM Firms," 1 (July 1991).

7.   *Engineering News Record*, "Top 100 CM Firms," 21 (June 1993): 33.

8.   Neil C. Churchill and Virginia L. Lewis, "The Five Stages of Small Business Growth," *Harvard Business Review* 61 (1983): 30–39.

V

Conclusions, Implications, and Recommendations

RESULTS ANALYSIS

The purpose of this study was to conduct an in-depth analysis of an African American-owned firmed, Don Todd Associates, Inc. In order to complete the case study, an interview protocol was used based on the Technical, Political and Cultural framework set forth by Noel Tichy.[1] The framework has eight components, which measure the three subsystems of an organization: technical, political, and cultural. A ninth dimension, "future," was added by the researcher.

The data obtained by the researcher from interviews with twelve employees of Don Todd Associates, Inc. and the analysis of the data was presented in Chapter Four. Following are the conclusions, implications, and recommendations for further research.

CONCLUSIONS

Analysis of Don Todd Associates, Inc.

Don Todd Associates Inc. (DTA) is a seventeen year old African American-owned firm that has a multi-ethnic staff. It is a project/construction management firm with major offices in Cherry Hill, New Jersey; New York City; and headquarters in San Francisco. The firm has grown from two employees in 1977 to 125 employees in 1994, and is ranked #58 in the Top 100 Construction Management firms by ENR. While the firm has experienced a substantial growth pattern with regard to both revenues and staff, it faces some serious challenges. The challenges include increased competition, decreased project opportunities, competitive hiring environment, and removal of the affirmative action program as a stimulation for new business.

The Tichy Technical, Political, Cultural Framework allowed for detailed analysis of the DTA past and projections about the future. Interviews of twelve employees and a review of company documents was completed using a questionnaire based on the eight components of the framework. The eight components are input (environment, history and resources); mission/strategy/objectives; tasks; prescribed organizational structure; people; organizational processes; emergent networks; outputs; and a ninth dimension of future, added by the researcher.

The research revealed that DTA has achieved many positive accomplishments, which could assist DTA in planning its future. DTA has a well defined market niche—construction management. The firm has remained focused and has been innovative and creative in the manner in which it has marketed its services. The DTA leadership has been clear to its staff regarding the company's goals and expectations. DTA has created a culture that allows individuals to be themselves, work creatively, and with the entrepreneurial spirit. This atmosphere has been supportive of acquiring and maintaining a multi-ethnic workforce where people feel their work is valued, as is their work performance and their relationship to the client. The firm and its staff has recognized the negative perception that many agencies and clients have regarding minority-owned firms and minority employees. The research revealed the employees believe some clients perceive minority firms as not as qualified as European American firms, and unable to accomplish the same volume and quality of work as their competitors. DTA has somewhat overcome this perception by emphasizing excellence in service, client relations, and networking. Based on the experience of the respondents, they believed that these perceptions will never be eradicated, and that DTA must continually cope with these and other negative perceptions. The respondents appeared prepared to do so.

The Tichy framework also revealed some areas needing improvement. While the firm has maintained a structure that was flexible enough to support the functional changes that may have been required in order to respond to environmental threats, the organizational structure and processes have not been communicated adequately throughout the organization. Employees below the vice presidential level are left in a quandary about organizational roles, responsibilities, and long-term goals. DTA could also benefit from delegating more responsibility clearly to its vice presidents and managers in a manner that integrates and empowers them. The firm may also benefit from a review of its financial performance for a clearer understanding of the fluctuation of financial performance. Finally, the firm needs to begin preparation for succession. Employees suspect a change is impending and they are concerned about the change because their faith is in the owner, Founder Donald J. Todd. This is not an unusual state for a firm that is still being managed by its Founder.

Clearly, DTA has been strongly influenced by the technical subsystem, with many changes in environmental opportunities and threats. The negative perceptions of minority-owned firms, the fluctuating economy and the affirmative action process have been key environmental elements influencing the technical subsystem. However, DTA has had strong leadership and management, with a strong culture that has values, beliefs, goals, and assumptions that have been developed in a manner that allows the multi-ethnic staff to embrace its culture and goals. Employees feel free to be themselves, bring their individual strength to the organization, form friendships in and out of their ethnic groups, and are challenged with a variety of project types. This type of open culture has been important in attracting and retaining individuals from different ethnic groups. Consequently, the cultural subsystem has remained constant, and assisted the organization in responding successfully to its challenges. DTA may benefit from capitalizing on its strengths in order to meet the challenges of the future.

The political system is the least developed of the three systems. This may be impacted by the presence of a strong Founder who has enjoyed successful leadership of the company. In order to prepare for its future DTA must begin to make preparation for an eventual change in leadership. Delegation of more authority and responsibility to vice presidents and managers, developing a management information system, and clear and consistent communication to all staff are tasks that would initiate this preparation. If the organization is to outlive its key managers, strengthening of the organization must begin immediately.

Effectiveness of Research Design

A qualitative design was used to analyze DTA. Specifically, a case study with a semi-structured, open-ended interview format was used, coupled with a review of relevant DTA documents. This design was very effective in describing how DTA has developed, the phases of the company's development, and highlighting important elements in the company's history. The information presented led to an in-depth study of the organization which would not have been possible with a quantitative design. However, the case study design does limit the generalization of the study.

The data was collected from a stratified self-selected sample. This allowed the researcher to interview individuals at all levels of the organization and varying lengths of service.

IMPLICATIONS

The implications of this research are threefold: emerging themes derived from the data, academic (organizational and cultural) significance, and possibilities for operational use.

Emerging Themes

DTA's founding was based on an open systems model that responded to *need* and *opportunity*. This model has continued to be the basis of DTA's system-wide operation. The Founder of the organization used the open systems model to form his organization and adapted it to the organization's operation. The model has now been adapted by the organization's staff and become part of the system. See figures 10 and 11.

The data revealed that, in 1977, Donald Todd was presented an *opportunity* to start a business in San Francisco. The San Francisco Clean Water Program had a *need* to hire consultants and meet

Figure 10

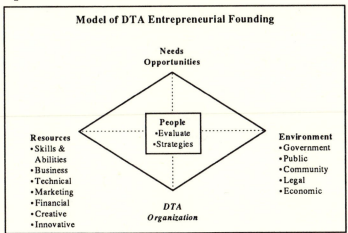

Figure 11

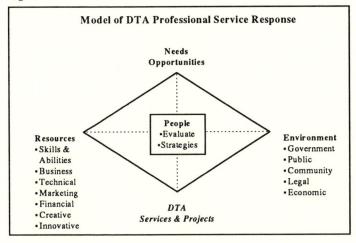

federal minority affirmative action goals simultaneously. Donald Todd became aware of the need, and seized it as an opportunity to start his own business. As the need arose, he began to hire people for the project. As new projects emerged and created opportunities for the organization, he hired additional staff. Departments, services and other offices were developed as the needs of the organization dictated or additional projects materialized. People were promoted in the organization as the need for such positions arose. Promotions were based primarily on the needs of the business and, secondly, on the need to reward an individual. The organization has continued to function in this manner.

Racism was viewed as the major obstacle to DTA's growth and success. Racism is defined as the tendency of people in other firms and agencies to perceive that minority-owned firms are incompetent, present inferior services, are second-rate, and function best on smaller projects or under supervision of European American-owned firms. Many people make a negative presumption about a firm upon hearing or seeing the word "minority."

This view of DTA was substantiated by respondents when European Americans questioned the authenticity of the company's minority ownership since the firm functioned so well. The assumption, in the frame of a question, was whether or not DTA was a minority "front" for a white owner. Another client indicated that he only uses DTA when he needs a good minority firm for a small job. There were many incidents that led the multi-ethnic respondents to believe that racism was the major obstacle to the company's success.

Negative perceptions of African Americans and other minorities are so pervasive in America, that this obstacle is unlikely to be overcome. As indicated by the Cose interviews, " . . . a ceiling exists for most African Americans that black skin is still equated by many in the business community with a lowering of standards, and that nothing much will change that."[2] However, the firm has successfully coped with this obstacle by maintaining an emphasis on excellence in product and client service. The firm has developed a culture that supports excellence and allows individuals and teams to perform at their best. It also encourages and cultivates an enabling process supportive of an entrepreneurial environment within the company.

Since the firm's inception, the goals of the organization have been very clear, although informally communicated. The goals have included provision of excellent service to clients, maintaining a profit and a multi-ethnic staff, and becoming an excellent construction management firm. These goals have been adopted by all staff and have become a part of the system.

The multi-ethnic staff embraced the goals of the organization. Hiring, rewards, and promotions were based on the individual performance. Work tasks were often interdependent, and performance is often measured by teams. Therefore, individuals assisted each other in getting the job done. Regardless of the individual's ethnicity, gender, or culture, acceptance was based on the individual's ability to further the company's goals.

The entrepreneurial attitude, that the Founder used to develop the organization, became pervasive throughout the organization. Consequently, different departments developed and expanded under the leadership of staff members who evolved through the system. DTA's leadership promoted an enabling process by developing the appropriate goals, providing individuals and groups with the necessary resources to achieve those goals, furnishing guidance in development and management of the entrepreneurial effort, and supplying space and flexibility.

The strong culture of the firm, as mentioned previously, supported DTA and its individuals in attaining their goals. The culture consists of multi-ethnic individuals who have developed mutual respect, support, and trust among themselves, as well as between the individuals and the organization. Hiring the best qualified individuals has led to the acquisition of a multi-ethnic staff. This heterogenous population has been able to collaborate and embrace unifying organizational assumptions regarding DTA's relationship with its internal and external environment, as well as the nature of human relations in this organization. Consequently, the challenges of the staff and its leaders have created a culture that copes with external adaptation or internal integration problems.

The fourth emerging theme speaks to the need of the organization to prepare for the "changing of the guard." The changes must occur whether it simply means distribution of more authority and responsibility to competent individuals in the firm, or succession planning that would call for Donald Todd to leave the presidency. Clearly, the organization has become too large to function with two individuals responsible for making all of the major decisions in the organization. Individuals independent of

Donald Todd and Daniel Anderson, representing DTA in the field, are leading groups of people and meeting with clients and owners. These individuals should be part of the organizational goal setting and major decision making. They must be empowered and prepared to manage the company in the absence of the owners. A deliberate structure for improvement of organizational processes, and training of vice presidents and managers, needs to be put in place.

The leaders of DTA also must develop strategies regarding the firm's future position. With the anticipated dilution of the future market due to encroachment of foreign-owned firms, and the increase in new and expanded construction management firms, DTA must to decide where its market will be. Two options available are the expansion of services into other states, and the global expansion of services. With the opening of markets in South Africa, Central America, and the Pacific Rim, DTA should investigate the needs and opportunities in these or other geographic areas.

Academic

The research indicated that this African American organization follows an evolutionary life cycle process as indicated in the literature. The life cycle does not fit a particular model but does follow a definite pattern. DTA can best be analyzed using the Tichy open systems model. The firm has been dynamic and changing since its inception. Technical, political, and cultural systems are in constant interaction, affecting the roles and expectations of both individuals and the organization. Consequently, these confirmations add to the existing body of knowledge on life cycle theory, and the theoretical framework on open systems models, and specifically that of Noel Tichy. Finally, this benchmark research adds to the sparse body of knowledge on African American-owned and led organizations.

There are three unique factors about DTA: It is an entrepreneurship, it is African American owned, and it has a multi-ethnic staff. The study indicated that DTA, by virtue of its growth and innovation, is an entrepreneurship. Innovation and creativity are demonstrated by the manner in which strategies have been created to continue to meet the need of clients. The fact that DTA is

African American owned has probably been the most significant difference of the organization. The ethnicity of its ownership brings it face to face with the obstacle of racism. The study demonstrates that an organization owned and led by African Americans can successfully serve a diversified population, and continue to grow despite this major obstacle.

With regard to culture, this research demonstrates that a multi-ethnic, heterogenous group can develop focused values, beliefs and goals, and contribute to the success of an organization. The research also demonstrates how a multi-ethnic staff can be acquired and maintained.

It may stimulate researchers to examine how minority-owned firms acquire and maintain multi-ethnic staff rather than focusing exclusively on large European American-owned firms. Perhaps there are lessons to be transferred from the management of minority-owned firms to that of large European American-owned firms instead of the reverse.

Additionally, there is some evidence that a culture that is led by African Americans, consisting primarily of African Americans and European Americans, may experience more tension than a culture that contains a more diverse ethnic population. This, also, warrants further research.

Operational

Operationally, the Tichy framework has proven to be an effective tool for examining this African American organization. It afforded the researcher the necessary information to answer the research questions and to analyze the organization. The framework is flexible enough to accommodate interviews, written questionnaires, document review and observation, and could be used to assist an organization with its strategic plan. It indicated DTA's strengths and weaknesses, which systems worked well, and which needed improvement. The TPC framework also indicated potential future problems and recommended necessary intervention.

FUTURE RESEARCH

It is hoped that this study will inspire further research in the area of African American entrepreneurship. Studies in this area may encourage other African Americans to initiate their own businesses. In addition, studies may assist in reducing the failure rate of African American-owned firms. The issues that are unique to African American-owned firms may be highlighted and a greater variety of solutions presented.

It is also hoped that this study will stimulate further research in the culture of African American-owned firms, specifically those that have a multi-ethnic staff. The current literature focuses primarily on multi-ethnic and multi-cultural staffs in European American-owned firms.

Comparison studies between African American-owned firms and firms from other ethnic groups would also be interesting and informative.

NOTES

1. Noel Tichy, "Managing Strategic Change: Technical, Political, and Cultural Dynamics," *Organizational Assessment and Change*, Edward Lawler III and Stanley E. Seashore, eds. (New York: John Wiley, 1983).

2. Ellis Cose, *The Rage of a Privileged Class*, (New York: HarperPerennial, 1993), p. 18.

Selected Bibliography

Adizes, Ichak. "Organizational Passages-Diagnosing and Treating Lifecycle Problems of an Organization." *Organizational Dynamics* 8 (1) (1979): 3–25.

Amit, Raphael, Lawrence Glosten, and Eitan Muller. "Challenges to Theory Development in Entrepreneurship Research." *Journal of Management Studies* 30 (1993): 815–834.

Bass, Bernard. "Leadership, Environment and Organization." In *The Handbook of Leadership*, ed. Bernard Bass and Ralph M. Stodgill. 3rd ed. New York: The Free Press, 1990. 563–594.

Bennis, Warren. *On Becoming a Leader*. Reading, MA: Addison-Wesley, 1989.

Blau, Peter. *On the Nature of Organizations*. New York: John Wiley, 1974.

Boeker, Warren. "Strategic Change: The Effects of Founding and History." *Academy of Management Journal* 32 (3) (1989): 489–515.

Borg, Walter R., and Damien Gall. *Educational Research: An Introduction*. White Plains: Longman, 1989.

Bygrave, William and Charles Hofer. "Researching Entrepreneurship." *Entrepreneurship Theory and Practice* 16 (3) (1992): 91–100.

Bygrave, William and Charles Hofer. "Theorizing About Entrepreneurship." *Entrepreneurship Theory and Practice*, (Winter 1991): 13–32.

Carland, James W., Frank Hoy, William R. Boulton, and Jo Ann C. Carland. "Differentiating Entrepreneurs from Small Business Owners: A Conceptualization." *Academy of Management Review* 9 (2) (1984): 354-359.

Carroll, John J. *The Filipino Manufacturing Entrepreneur*. Ithaca: Cornell University Press, 1965.

Churchill, Neil C. and Virginia L. Lewis. "The Five Stages of Small Business Growth." *Harvard Business Review* 61 (3) (1983): 30–39.

Cole, Arthur. *Business Enterprise in its Social Setting.* Cambridge: Harvard University Press, 1959.Cose, Ellis. *The Rage of a Privileged Class.* New York: Harper Perenial, 1993.

Davis, George and Glegg Watson. *Black Life in Corporate America.* Garden City, NY: Doubleday, 1982.

Deal, Terrence E. and Allan A. Kennedy. *Corporate Cultures: The Rites and Rituals of Corporate Life.* Reading, MA: Addison-Wesley Publishing Company, 1982.

Denison, Daniel. *Corporate Culture and Organizational Effectiveness.* New York: John Wiley & Sons, 1990.

Dickens, Floyd Jr. and Jacqueline B. Dickens. *The Black Manager: Making it in the Corporate World.* New York: AMACOM, 1991.

Dorf, Matthew. "NYC Kills Set-Aside Program." *Set-Aside Alert* 1 (23) (1994): 1.

Drucker, Peter F. "The Coming of the New Organization." *The Best of Harvard Business Review* (1991): 3–11.

Drucker, Peter F. *Innovation and Entrepreneurship: Practice and Principles.* New York: Harper & Row, 1985.

Dubois, W.E.B. *The Negro in Business.* Reprint ed., New York: AMS Press, 1971 [1899].

Dyer, W. Gibbs. *Strategies for Managing Change.* Reading, MA: Addison-Wesley, 1984.

Engineering News Record, 1 July, 1991, "Top 100 CM Firms."

Engineering News Record, 21 June 1993, p. 33. "Top 100 CM Firms."

Engineering News Record, 31 January 1994, p. 45. "Special Report: Forecast '94."

Engineering News Record, 4 April 1994, pp. 28–29. "Turner Bites Bullet Now to Improve Profitability and Productivity Ahead."

Fernandez, John P. *The Diversity Advantage.* Lexington, MA: Lexington Books, 1993.

Fiscal 1993 Audit Report of Don Todd Associates, Inc. Don Todd Associates, Inc., 1994. Financial Audit.

Flamholtz, Eric G. "Toward a Holistic Model of Organizational Effectiveness and Organizational Development at Different Stages of Growth." *Human Resource Development Quarterly* 1 (2) (1990): 109–127.

Frey, Scott R. " Need for Achievement, Entrepreneurship, and Economic Growth: A Critique of the McClelland Thesis." *Social Science Journal* 21 (2) (1984): 125–134.

Gartner, William. "Who is an Entrepreneur? Is the Wrong Question." *EntrepreneurshipTheory and Practice* 13 (4) (1989): 47–68.

Glade, William P. "Approaches to a Theory of Entrepreneurial Formation." *Explorations in Entrepreneurial History* 4 (1967): 245–259.

Glenn, Gwendolyn. "Getting Down to Case Studies." *Black Issues In Higher Education* 10 (22) (1993): 26–27.

Greiner, Larry E. "Evolution and Revolution as Organizations Grow." *Harvard Business Review* 50 (4) (1972): 37-46.

Gupta, Udayan and Jeanne Saddler. "Financing Prospects for Black Businesses Remain Poor." *The Wall Street Journal*, 16 May 1994, B2.

Hagen, Everett. *On the Theory of Social Change*. Homewood, IL: Dorsey Press, 1962.

Harris, Adrienne S. "Hot Kidpreneur Programs." *Black Enterprise* (February 1994): 177–182.

Higginbotham, Leon. *In the Matter of Color: The Colonial Period*. New York: Oxford University Press, 1978.

Hirsch, Robert, Richard Neilson, and Michael Peters. "Intrapraneurship Strategy for Internal Markets--Corporate, Non-profit and Government Institution Cases." *Strategic Management Journal* 6 (1985): 181.

Ichniowski, Timothy. "The Main Men on Public Works." *Engineering News Record*, 6 September 1993, 24.

Johnston, William and Arnold Packer. *Workforce 2000:Work and Workers for the Twenty-First Century*. U.S. Department of Labor. Indianapolis: Hudson Institute, 1987.

Katz, Daniel and Robert L. Kahn. *The Social Psychology of Organizations*. New York: John Wiley, 1966.

Kent, Calvin A., Donald L. Sexton, and Karl H. Vesper. *Encyclopedia of Entrepreneurship*. Englewood Cliffs, NJ: Prentice-Hall, 1982.

Kilar, J. Q. "Black Entrepreneurs in the Michigan Lumber Towns." *Negro History Bulletin* (1983): 52–53.

Kimberly, John R. "Issues in the Creation of Organizations: Initiation, Innovation and Institutionalization." *Academy of Management* 22 (1979): 437-457.

Kimberly, John R. and Robert H. Miles, ed. "The Life Cycle Analogy and the Study of Organizations." *The Organizational Life Cycle - Social and Behavioral Science Series*. San Francisco: Jossey-Bass, 1980.

Kimberly, John R. and Robert H. Miles, ed. "Social and Behavioral Science Series." *The Organizational Life Cycle*. Social and Behavioral Science Series. San Francisco: Jossey-Bass, 1980.

Kimbro, Dennis and Napoleon Hill. *Think* and *Grow Rich: A Black Choice*. New York: Ballentine Books, 1991.

Krizan, William G., Harry. Bradford, and Susan W. Setzer. "Scent of Recovery is in the Air. *Engineering News Record*, 31 January 1994, 73.

Leung, Chi-Sun Benjamin. *Diversity Training in the Corporate World of America: A Look at the Heartland of America*. Warrensburg, MO: Central Missouri State University, 1995.

Lippitt, Gordon and Warren Schmidt. "Crises in a Developing Organization." *Harvard Business Review* 45 (6) (1967): 102-112.

Low, Murray and Ian C. MacMillan. "Entrepreneurship: Past Research and Future Challenges." *Journal of Management* 14 (1988): 139–161.

Lyles, Carole Y. "People of Color: Finding Voice." *OD Practitioner* (Winter 1993): 11–16.

McCall, Nathan. "How Herman Russell Built His Business...Brick by Brick." *Black Enterprise*, June, 1987: 176-184.

McClelland, David. *The Achieving Society*. Princeton: D. Van Nostrand, 1961.

Miles, Matthew, and A. Michael Huberman. *Qualitative Data Analysis: A Sourcebook of New Methods*. Newbury Park, CA: Sage, 1984.

Morgan, Edmund. *American Slavery, American Freedom: Ordeal of Colonial Virginia*. New York: Norton, 1975.

Ndulue, John Chika Agboso. "Urban Black Adaptation and Successful Entrepreneurship in Chicago: An Extended Cast Study of a Black-owned and Operated Construction Firm." Ph.D. diss., University of Illinois, 1985.

Neilson, Richard, Michael Peters, and Robert Hirisch. "Intrapreneurship Strategy for Internal Markets-Corporate, Nonprofit and Government Institution Cases." *Strategic Management Journal* 6 (1985):181.

Principal's Report (12) (1993). "Exercising Leadership: California Principals Prepare to Rebound from the Recession."

Quinn, Robert and Kim Cameron. "Organizational Life Cycles and Shifting Criteria of Effectiveness: Some Preliminary Evidence." *Management Science* 29 (1) (1983): 33-51.

Ragsdale, Lincoln Johnson. "Minority Entrepreneurship: Profiling an African-American Entrepreneur." Ph.D. diss., The Union for Experimenting Colleges and Universities, 1989.

Rhinehart, Milton Duncan. "Cultural Diversity at Work and Its Effect on Organization Communication and Conflict." Ph.D. diss., University of Colorado at Boulder, 1994.

Rosen, Michael J. "The Life Cycle Development of a Voluntary Organization: A Case Analysis of Uncertainty and Change." Ph.D. diss., University of Massachusetts, 1986.

Saddler, Jeanne. "Young Risk-Takers Push the Business Envelope." *The Wall Street Journal*, 12 May 1994, B1.

Samuels, Allison. "Succession Planning in African-American Businesses." *Upscale*, (March, 1994): 34–38.

Say, Jean Baptiste. *The Production, Distribution and Consumption of Wealth*. French translation from 4th Edition. Boston: Wells & Lily, 1921.

Schein, Edgar. "Coming to a New Awareness of Organizational Culture." *Sloan Management Review* 25 (2) (1984): 3–16.

Schein, Edgar H. "The Role of the Founder in the Creation of Organizational Culture." *Organizational Dynamics* (Summer 1983): 13–28.

Schumpeter, Joseph. "Creative Response in Economic History." *The Journal of Economic History* VII (2) (1947): 149–159.

Schumpeter, Joseph. *The Theory of Economic Development*. Translation by R. Opie. Cambridge: Harvard University Press, 1934.

Senge, Peter M. *The Fifth Discipline*. New York: Doubleday/Currency, 1990.

Shapero, Albert and Lisa Sokol. "The Social Dimensions of Entrepreneurship." In *Encyclopedia of Entrepreneurship*, ed. Donald L. Sexton, Calvin A. Kent and Karl Vesper. Englewood Cliffs, NJ: Prentice-Hall, 1982.

Stacey, Michael John. "The Life Cycle of a Small Family-Run Entrepreneurial Organization: A Case Analysis of Change and Growth." Ph.D. diss., University of Massachusetts, 1991.

Thomas, Roosevelt R. Jr. *Beyond Race and Gender: Unleashing the Power of Your Total Workforce by Managing Diversity*. New York: AMACOM, 1991.

Thomas Jr., R. Roosevelt, Tracy Irving Gray, Jr. and Marjorie Woodroof. *Differences Do Make a Differences*. Atlanta: The American Institute for Managing Diversity Inc., 1992.

Tichy, Noel. "Managing Strategic Change: Technical, Political, and Cultural Dynamics." *Organizational Assessment and Change*, ed. Edward Lawler III and Stanley E. Seashore. New York: John Wiley & Sons, 1983.

Tichy, Noel. "Problem Cycles in Organizations and the Management of Change." In *The Organizational Life Cycle*, ed. by John R. Kimberly and Robert H. Miles. San Francisco: Jossey Bass, 1987.

Tichy, Noel and Mary Anne Devanna. *The Transformational Leader*. New York: John Wiley, 1986.

Timmons, Jeffrey. *New Venture Creation*. 3rd ed., Homewood, IL: Irwin, 1990.

Todd, Gwendolyn Powell. "DTA Client Satisfaction Survey." San Francisco, Don Todd Associates, Inc., 1994.

Todd, Gwendolyn Powell. "The Gift of a Good Example." *Minorities and Women In Business* (May 1993): 22–23.

Ubben, Gerald C., and Larry W. Hughes. *The Principal: Creative Leadership for Effective Schools*. Newton, Massachusetts: Allyn and Bacon, 1987.

Venable, Abraham. *Building Black Business*. New York: Crowell, 1972.

Vesper, Karl H. *New Venture Strategies*. Englewood Cliffs, NJ: Prentice-Hall,1980.

Whetten, David A. "Organizational Decline: A Neglected Topic in Organizational Science." *Academy of Management Review* 5 (4) (1980): 577–588.

Yin, Robert K. *Case Study Research*. Newbury Park, California: Sage, 1989.

Index